ClipCharm

for Beginners

A Step-by-Step Guide in Microsoft 365

Kiet Huynh

Table of Contents

CHAPTER I
Introduction to ClipCharm and Microsoft 365

1.1 What is ClipCharm?

1.1.1 Overview and Purpose

In today's fast-paced digital world, efficiency and productivity are crucial. ClipCharm, an innovative tool within the Microsoft 365 ecosystem, aims to streamline workflows and enhance productivity by simplifying the process of creating, managing, and sharing multimedia content. But what exactly is ClipCharm, and why is it gaining traction among Microsoft 365 users?

Overview of ClipCharm ClipCharm is a versatile application designed to work seamlessly within the Microsoft 365 suite. It serves as a powerful content creation and management tool, allowing users to create, edit, and organize video clips and multimedia content with ease. Whether you are preparing a presentation, designing a training module, or sharing important updates with your team, ClipCharm offers the functionalities to make your tasks more efficient and visually engaging.

Purpose of ClipCharm The primary purpose of ClipCharm is to empower users to create high-quality multimedia content without needing advanced technical skills. By integrating directly with Microsoft 365, ClipCharm leverages the familiar interface and functionalities of the suite, making it accessible for both novice and experienced users. Here are some of the key purposes and benefits of using ClipCharm:

1. Streamlined Content Creation: ClipCharm simplifies the process of creating video clips, enabling users to produce professional-looking content quickly. With its intuitive drag-and-drop interface, users can easily combine various multimedia elements, such as images, videos, and audio, to create compelling clips.

2. Enhanced Collaboration: In a collaborative environment, ClipCharm shines by allowing multiple users to work on the same project simultaneously. This real-time collaboration feature ensures that team members can contribute their expertise, making the content creation process more dynamic and efficient.

3. Seamless Integration: As part of the Microsoft 365 ecosystem, ClipCharm integrates seamlessly with other applications like Word, Excel, PowerPoint, and Teams. This integration facilitates the embedding of video clips into documents, spreadsheets, presentations, and communication channels, enhancing the overall effectiveness of your content.

4. Efficient Content Management: ClipCharm offers robust content management features, including tagging, categorization, and search functionalities. These features ensure that users can easily organize and retrieve their multimedia assets, saving valuable time and effort.

5. Customization and Flexibility: With ClipCharm, users have access to a variety of templates and customization options, allowing them to tailor their content to specific needs and preferences. This flexibility ensures that the created content aligns with the brand identity and messaging of the organization.

6. Improved Engagement: Video content is known to capture attention and improve engagement. ClipCharm enables users to create visually appealing and engaging content that can be used for various purposes, such as marketing campaigns, internal communications, and educational materials.

Key Features of ClipCharm To understand the full potential of ClipCharm, it's essential to explore its key features. These features are designed to simplify the content creation process and enhance the overall user experience. Some of the standout features include:

1. User-Friendly Interface: ClipCharm's interface is designed to be intuitive and user-friendly. Even users with minimal technical skills can navigate through the application and create content effortlessly.

2. Drag-and-Drop Functionality: The drag-and-drop feature allows users to easily add multimedia elements to their clips. Whether it's importing images, videos, or audio files, ClipCharm makes the process seamless.

3. Templates and Themes: ClipCharm offers a variety of templates and themes that users can choose from. These pre-designed templates provide a head start in creating professional-looking content, saving users time and effort.

4. Real-Time Collaboration: Collaboration is a key aspect of ClipCharm. Multiple users can work on the same project simultaneously, providing real-time feedback and contributions. This feature is particularly useful for teams working on collaborative projects.

5. Integration with Microsoft 365 Apps: One of ClipCharm's most significant advantages is its integration with other Microsoft 365 applications. Users can easily embed their clips into Word documents, Excel spreadsheets, PowerPoint presentations, and Teams meetings.

6. Advanced Editing Tools: ClipCharm provides a range of editing tools that allow users to customize their clips. From trimming and cropping to adding transitions and effects, these tools enable users to create polished and professional content.

7. Content Management System: The built-in content management system helps users organize their clips efficiently. Features like tagging, categorization, and search functionality make it easy to locate and manage multimedia assets.

8. Export and Sharing Options: Once the content is created, ClipCharm offers various export and sharing options. Users can export their clips in different formats and resolutions or share them directly through Microsoft 365 applications.

9. Analytics and Insights: ClipCharm provides analytics and insights into the performance of the created content. Users can track metrics like views, engagement, and feedback, allowing them to measure the effectiveness of their clips.

Conclusion

ClipCharm represents a significant advancement in the realm of content creation and management within the Microsoft 365 suite. By offering a user-friendly interface, seamless integration, and powerful features, ClipCharm enables users to produce high-quality multimedia content efficiently. Whether you are an individual user or part of a collaborative team, ClipCharm provides the tools you need to create, manage, and share engaging content that meets your specific needs.

As you delve deeper into this book, you will discover step-by-step guides, tips, and best practices to help you harness the full potential of ClipCharm. From the basics of getting started to advanced techniques and features, this book aims to equip you with the knowledge and skills to become proficient in using ClipCharm within Microsoft 365.

1.1.2 Key Features

ClipCharm is a powerful tool designed to enhance productivity and streamline content creation within the Microsoft 365 ecosystem. This section delves into the key features that make ClipCharm an indispensable asset for users looking to optimize their workflow and improve collaboration.

User-Friendly Interface

One of the most striking features of ClipCharm is its intuitive and user-friendly interface. Designed with ease of use in mind, the interface allows users to quickly navigate through the various functionalities without a steep learning curve. The dashboard provides a clear overview of all available tools and options, ensuring that even beginners can start using ClipCharm effectively right away.

Comprehensive Clip Library

ClipCharm boasts a comprehensive clip library that allows users to store, organize, and manage all their clips in one place. This library supports various types of content, including text, images, videos, and links, making it a versatile tool for all kinds of projects. Users can easily categorize and tag their clips, making retrieval simple and efficient. The ability to search and filter clips by keywords or tags further enhances the user experience, allowing for quick access to needed resources.

Easy Clip Creation and Editing

Creating and editing clips in ClipCharm is a straightforward process. Users can easily create new clips from scratch or import existing content. The editing tools are robust, offering features such as text formatting, image editing, and video trimming. Additionally, users can customize their clips with annotations, highlights, and comments, making it easy to convey specific messages or instructions. The ability to save drafts and work on clips incrementally ensures that users can maintain a steady workflow without losing their progress.

Seamless Integration with Microsoft 365

One of the standout features of ClipCharm is its seamless integration with Microsoft 365. This integration allows users to easily incorporate ClipCharm into their existing workflows within Microsoft applications such as Word, Excel, PowerPoint, and Teams. For instance, users can insert clips directly into documents, spreadsheets, and presentations, or share them during team meetings. This interoperability enhances the overall utility of ClipCharm, making it a valuable addition to the Microsoft 365 suite.

Collaborative Tools

ClipCharm is designed with collaboration in mind. The platform offers several features that facilitate teamwork and collective content creation. Users can share clips with colleagues, assign tasks, and provide feedback through comments and annotations. Real-time editing and updating ensure that all team members are always on the same page, reducing the risk of miscommunication and errors. The ability to set permissions and access levels adds an extra layer of security, ensuring that only authorized personnel can make changes to critical content.

Automation Capabilities

Automation is a key feature that sets ClipCharm apart from other content management tools. Users can automate repetitive tasks such as clip organization, tagging, and distribution. For example, clips can be automatically categorized based on predefined rules or shared with specific team members at scheduled intervals. This not only saves time but also ensures consistency and accuracy in content management. Advanced users can set up custom automation workflows to meet their unique needs, further enhancing productivity.

Robust Security Features

Security is a top priority for ClipCharm, especially given the sensitive nature of the content it handles. The platform employs robust security measures to protect user data and ensure compliance with industry standards. Features such as data encryption, secure access controls, and regular security updates safeguard against unauthorized access and data breaches. Additionally, ClipCharm offers audit trails and activity logs, allowing administrators to monitor usage and detect any suspicious activity.

Customization Options

ClipCharm provides extensive customization options, allowing users to tailor the platform to their specific needs. Users can customize the interface by rearranging widgets, adjusting display settings, and creating custom templates. Additionally, ClipCharm supports a variety of plugins and extensions, enabling users to add new functionalities or integrate with other tools they use. This flexibility ensures that ClipCharm can adapt to different workflows and preferences, making it a versatile solution for various industries and use cases.

Detailed Analytics and Reporting

Understanding how clips are used and their impact on productivity is crucial for continuous improvement. ClipCharm offers detailed analytics and reporting features that provide insights into clip usage, user engagement, and overall effectiveness. Users can generate reports on metrics such as the number of clips created, shared, and viewed, as well as the time spent on each clip. These insights help users identify areas for improvement, optimize their content strategies, and demonstrate the value of ClipCharm to stakeholders.

Mobile Compatibility

In today's fast-paced work environment, having access to tools on the go is essential. ClipCharm is fully compatible with mobile devices, allowing users to create, edit, and share clips from their smartphones or tablets. The mobile app offers the same functionalities as the desktop version, ensuring a seamless user experience across all devices. This mobility ensures that users can stay productive and connected, regardless of their location.

Scalability

ClipCharm is designed to scale with the needs of its users. Whether you are an individual user, a small team, or a large organization, ClipCharm can accommodate your requirements. The platform supports multiple users and projects, making it easy to manage a growing volume of content and collaboration activities. Additionally, ClipCharm's cloud-based infrastructure ensures that it can handle increased demand without compromising performance.

Continuous Updates and Support

ClipCharm is committed to continuous improvement and user satisfaction. The platform regularly releases updates that introduce new features, enhance existing functionalities, and address any issues. Users have access to a comprehensive support system, including online tutorials, help documentation, and customer service. The ClipCharm community also offers a platform for users to share tips, ask questions, and collaborate on best practices.

Templates and Pre-Built Content

To help users get started quickly, ClipCharm offers a variety of templates and pre-built content. These templates cover a range of use cases, such as meeting agendas, project plans, and marketing materials. Users can customize these templates to suit their specific needs, saving time and ensuring consistency. The availability of pre-built content also serves as inspiration, helping users to explore new ways of utilizing ClipCharm.

Integration with Third-Party Applications

In addition to its seamless integration with Microsoft 365, ClipCharm supports integration with a wide range of third-party applications. This includes popular tools such as Slack, Trello, and Asana, allowing users to incorporate ClipCharm into their broader workflow ecosystem. These integrations enhance the versatility of ClipCharm, making it a central hub for content management and collaboration.

Offline Access

ClipCharm recognizes that users may not always have reliable internet access. To address this, the platform offers offline access, allowing users to create and edit clips without an internet connection. Changes made offline are automatically synced once the user reconnects to the internet, ensuring that their work is not lost. This feature is particularly useful for users who frequently travel or work in remote locations.

Multi-Language Support

In a globalized work environment, language support is crucial. ClipCharm offers multi-language support, allowing users to switch between different languages based on their preferences. This ensures that non-English speakers can use the platform effectively, enhancing its accessibility and usability. The availability of localized help resources and customer support further supports international users.

Environmental Sustainability

ClipCharm is committed to environmental sustainability. The platform is designed to reduce paper usage by digitizing content creation and management processes. This not only saves trees but also reduces the carbon footprint associated with printing and physical storage. ClipCharm's cloud-based infrastructure is optimized for energy efficiency, further contributing to its sustainability goals.

Conclusion

The key features of ClipCharm make it a powerful tool for enhancing productivity, collaboration, and content management within Microsoft 365. From its user-friendly interface and comprehensive clip library to its robust security features and automation capabilities, ClipCharm offers a range of functionalities that cater to the needs of various users. Its seamless integration with Microsoft 365 and third-party applications, combined with continuous updates and support, ensures that ClipCharm remains a valuable asset for individuals and organizations alike.

By leveraging these features, users can streamline their workflows, improve collaboration, and achieve better outcomes in their projects. As we explore further chapters in this guide, we will delve deeper into how to utilize these features effectively, providing step-by-step instructions and best practices to help you get the most out of ClipCharm in Microsoft 365.

1.2 Introduction to Microsoft 365

1.2.1 Overview of Microsoft 365

 Microsoft 365, formerly known as Office 365, is a suite of cloud-based productivity and collaboration tools developed by Microsoft. It encompasses a variety of applications and services designed to improve efficiency, communication, and collaboration within organizations of all sizes. Microsoft 365 includes well-known applications such as Word, Excel, PowerPoint, Outlook, and Teams, along with newer services like OneDrive, SharePoint, and Yammer. This comprehensive suite is designed to meet the diverse needs of modern businesses, providing tools that cater to both individual productivity and team collaboration.

Microsoft 365 is built on a foundation of cloud computing, which means that all applications and services are hosted on Microsoft's servers and accessed via the internet. This cloud-based approach offers numerous benefits, including the ability to access files and applications from any device with an internet connection, seamless updates and maintenance, and robust security measures to protect sensitive data. The suite is available through a subscription model, offering various plans tailored to different user needs, from individual users and small businesses to large enterprises.

Key Applications and Services in Microsoft 365

Word

Microsoft Word is a word processing application that allows users to create, edit, and format text documents. It is widely used for creating reports, letters, resumes, and other professional documents. Word offers a variety of templates, formatting tools, and collaborative features that enable multiple users to work on a document simultaneously.

Excel

Microsoft Excel is a powerful spreadsheet application used for data analysis, visualization, and management. It is commonly used for financial modeling, budgeting, and data tracking. Excel provides a range of functions, charts, and pivot tables to help users analyze data and make informed decisions.

PowerPoint

Microsoft PowerPoint is a presentation application used to create slideshows for meetings, conferences, and educational purposes. PowerPoint offers a wide array of design tools, animation effects, and multimedia integration options to help users create engaging and visually appealing presentations.

Outlook

Microsoft Outlook is an email and calendar application that helps users manage their communication and schedules. Outlook integrates with other Microsoft 365 applications, allowing users to send and receive emails, schedule meetings, and manage tasks from a single platform.

Teams

Microsoft Teams is a collaboration platform that combines chat, video conferencing, file sharing, and app integration. Teams is designed to facilitate communication and collaboration among team members, whether they are in the same office or working remotely. It supports real-time collaboration on documents, project management, and virtual meetings.

OneDrive

Microsoft OneDrive is a cloud storage service that allows users to store, sync, and share files. OneDrive provides users with access to their files from any device with an internet connection, making it easy to collaborate with others and ensure that important documents are always available.

SharePoint

Microsoft SharePoint is a web-based collaboration and document management platform. It enables organizations to create, store, and manage content in a centralized location. SharePoint supports team collaboration, content management, and workflow automation, making it an essential tool for managing information and processes within an organization.

Benefits of Cloud-Based Services

Microsoft 365's cloud-based architecture offers several advantages over traditional, on-premises software solutions. Some of the key benefits include:

Accessibility

With Microsoft 365, users can access their files and applications from any device with an internet connection. This flexibility allows employees to work from anywhere, whether they are in the office, at home, or on the go. It also supports the growing trend of remote work and flexible work arrangements.

Automatic Updates

Microsoft 365 automatically updates applications and services, ensuring that users always have access to the latest features and security enhancements. This eliminates the need for manual updates and reduces the risk of using outdated software.

Scalability

Microsoft 365 offers a range of subscription plans that can be tailored to the needs of different organizations. This scalability makes it easy for businesses to add or remove users, upgrade plans, and access additional features as their needs evolve.

Security

Microsoft 365 includes robust security measures to protect sensitive data and ensure compliance with industry regulations. Features such as data encryption, multi-factor authentication, and advanced threat protection help safeguard information and prevent unauthorized access.

Collaboration

Microsoft 365 is designed to enhance collaboration and communication among team members. Tools like Teams, SharePoint, and OneDrive facilitate real-time collaboration on documents, project management, and communication, making it easier for teams to work together and achieve their goals.

Subscription Plans

Microsoft 365 offers a variety of subscription plans to meet the needs of different users and organizations. Some of the most common plans include:

Microsoft 365 Personal

Designed for individual users, this plan includes access to the core Microsoft 365 applications (Word, Excel, PowerPoint, Outlook) and 1 TB of OneDrive storage. It also includes premium features such as advanced security and technical support.

Microsoft 365 Family

This plan is designed for families and includes access for up to six users. Each user gets access to the core Microsoft 365 applications, 1 TB of OneDrive storage, and premium features. The Family plan is ideal for households with multiple users who need access to Microsoft 365.

Microsoft 365 Business Basic

Designed for small businesses, this plan includes access to web-based versions of the core Microsoft 365 applications, as well as Teams, OneDrive, and SharePoint. It also includes business email and calendar services.

Microsoft 365 Business Standard

This plan includes access to both web-based and desktop versions of the core Microsoft 365 applications, as well as Teams, OneDrive, and SharePoint. It also includes business email and calendar services, making it ideal for small to medium-sized businesses.

Microsoft 365 Business Premium

Designed for businesses with more advanced needs, this plan includes all the features of the Business Standard plan, as well as advanced security and device management tools. It is ideal for organizations that require enhanced security and compliance features.

Microsoft 365 Enterprise

This plan is designed for large organizations and includes advanced security, compliance, and productivity features. It offers access to the full range of Microsoft 365 applications and services, as well as additional tools for managing large-scale deployments. *Conclusion*

Microsoft 365 is a comprehensive suite of productivity and collaboration tools designed to meet the diverse needs of modern organizations. Its cloud-based architecture, robust security features, and seamless integration with tools like ClipCharm make it an essential platform for improving efficiency, communication, and collaboration. Whether you are an individual user, a small business, or a large enterprise, Microsoft 365 provides the tools and features you need to succeed in today's fast-paced, digital world.

1.2.2 Integration with ClipCharm

ClipCharm is an innovative tool that seamlessly integrates with Microsoft 365, enhancing the suite's capabilities and offering users a more dynamic and efficient way to manage their content and workflows. In this section, we will explore how ClipCharm integrates with various Microsoft 365 applications and how you can leverage this integration to optimize your productivity.

Understanding ClipCharm Integration

The integration between ClipCharm and Microsoft 365 is designed to be intuitive and user-friendly, allowing users to quickly and easily access ClipCharm's features within the familiar Microsoft 365 environment. This integration streamlines the workflow, making it easier to create, manage, and share content without having to switch between different applications.

Integration with Microsoft Word

One of the most significant integrations of ClipCharm is with Microsoft Word. Word is widely used for creating and editing documents, and ClipCharm enhances this experience by allowing users to insert pre-made clips directly into their documents. Here's how it works:

1. Accessing ClipCharm in Word: Once ClipCharm is installed and configured, you can access it directly from the Word ribbon. A ClipCharm tab will appear, giving you quick access to your library of clips.

2. Inserting Clips: You can browse through your clips and insert them into your document with a single click. This is particularly useful for repetitive content such as standard paragraphs, legal disclaimers, or any other frequently used text.

3. Editing Clips: If you need to make adjustments to a clip, you can do so directly within Word. The changes will be saved in your ClipCharm library, ensuring that you always have the most up-to-date version available.

Integration with Microsoft Excel

ClipCharm's integration with Microsoft Excel is another powerful feature that can significantly enhance your productivity. Excel is essential for managing data and performing calculations, and ClipCharm can help streamline these processes:

1. Inserting Data Clips: Just like in Word, you can insert data clips into your Excel spreadsheets. This is particularly useful for standard data sets, formulas, or any other content that you use regularly.

2. Template Management: ClipCharm allows you to create and manage templates within Excel. This can save you a lot of time when setting up new spreadsheets, as you can start with a pre-configured template that includes all the necessary formatting and data structures.

3. Collaboration Features: ClipCharm makes it easier to share and collaborate on Excel files. You can share clips with your team, ensuring that everyone has access to the same data and templates.

Integration with Microsoft PowerPoint

PowerPoint is a powerful tool for creating presentations, and ClipCharm's integration can help you create more engaging and professional presentations with less effort:

1. Inserting Slide Clips: You can save entire slides or groups of slides as clips in ClipCharm. This allows you to quickly insert these slides into new presentations, ensuring consistency and saving time.

2. Design Templates: ClipCharm can store design templates, making it easy to apply a consistent look and feel to all your presentations. You can create custom templates that match your branding and insert them into new presentations with a single click.

3. Multimedia Clips: ClipCharm supports multimedia content, so you can store and insert images, videos, and other media files directly into your PowerPoint slides.

Integration with Microsoft Outlook

Email is a critical component of most business communications, and ClipCharm's integration with Outlook can help you manage your emails more efficiently:

1. Email Templates: ClipCharm allows you to create and store email templates, which you can then insert into your emails with a single click. This is particularly useful for standard responses, marketing emails, and other repetitive communications.

2. Signature Management: You can create and manage multiple email signatures in ClipCharm, making it easy to switch between different signatures depending on the context of your email.

3. Attachment Management: ClipCharm can help you manage email attachments by storing frequently used documents and files, which you can then attach to your emails directly from the ClipCharm library.

Integration with Microsoft Teams

Microsoft Teams is a powerful collaboration tool, and ClipCharm's integration can help you manage your team's content more effectively:

1. Content Sharing: You can share clips directly within Teams, making it easy to share standard documents, templates, and other content with your team.

2. Meeting Notes: ClipCharm can help you manage meeting notes by allowing you to save and share standard note templates. This ensures that all your meetings are documented consistently and professionally.

3. Task Management: You can use ClipCharm to create and manage task templates, which can then be assigned to team members within Teams. This helps streamline your workflow and ensures that everyone knows what they need to do.

Integration with OneDrive

OneDrive is Microsoft's cloud storage service, and ClipCharm's integration allows you to manage your clips more effectively:

1. Cloud Storage: ClipCharm can save your clips directly to OneDrive, ensuring that they are always backed up and accessible from anywhere.

2. File Sharing: You can share clips stored in OneDrive with others, making it easy to collaborate on documents and other content.

3. Version Control: ClipCharm's integration with OneDrive includes version control features, allowing you to track changes and revert to previous versions if necessary.

Integration with SharePoint

SharePoint is a powerful tool for managing content and collaboration within an organization, and ClipCharm's integration can enhance its capabilities:

1. Document Management: You can use ClipCharm to manage and share standard documents within SharePoint, ensuring that everyone has access to the latest versions.

2. Content Libraries: ClipCharm allows you to create and manage content libraries within SharePoint, making it easy to organize and find the content you need.

3. Collaboration Features: ClipCharm's integration with SharePoint includes powerful collaboration features, allowing you to work on documents with others in real time.

Conclusion

The integration of ClipCharm with Microsoft 365 offers a wide range of benefits that can significantly enhance your productivity and streamline your workflows. By leveraging the power of ClipCharm within the familiar Microsoft 365 environment, you can create, manage, and share content more efficiently, ensuring that you and your team can focus on what really matters.

Whether you are creating documents in Word, managing data in Excel, preparing presentations in PowerPoint, sending emails in Outlook, collaborating in Teams, or managing files in OneDrive and SharePoint, ClipCharm provides the tools you need to work more effectively. By understanding and utilizing these integrations, you can unlock the full potential of both ClipCharm and Microsoft 365, transforming the way you work and collaborate.

1.3 Benefits of Using ClipCharm in Microsoft 365

1.3.1 Improved Productivity

Using ClipCharm within Microsoft 365 offers numerous benefits that can significantly improve productivity for both individual users and teams. This section delves into how ClipCharm can enhance productivity by streamlining workflows, reducing redundant tasks, and fostering better collaboration.

Streamlined Workflows

One of the primary ways ClipCharm improves productivity is by streamlining workflows. ClipCharm allows users to create, store, and manage reusable clips of information that can be quickly inserted into various documents, emails, and presentations. This feature is particularly beneficial for tasks that require repetitive information, such as customer responses, standard operating procedures, or recurring project updates.

For instance, instead of manually typing out the same response to multiple customer inquiries, a user can create a clip with the standard response and use ClipCharm to insert it with just a few clicks. This not only saves time but also ensures consistency in communication.

Time Savings

The time saved by using ClipCharm can be substantial. According to various productivity studies, employees spend a significant portion of their time on repetitive tasks. By leveraging ClipCharm, users can reduce the time spent on these tasks, freeing up more time for strategic, high-value activities.

For example, consider a marketing professional who frequently sends out proposals to potential clients. With ClipCharm, they can create a library of commonly used proposal sections, such as company introductions, service descriptions, and case studies. When drafting a new proposal, they can simply insert these clips instead of rewriting the content each time. This efficiency can reduce the proposal creation time by half or more, allowing the professional to focus on customizing the proposal to the client's specific needs or working on other marketing initiatives.

Consistency and Accuracy

Another critical aspect of productivity is ensuring consistency and accuracy in the information shared across the organization. ClipCharm helps maintain this consistency by allowing users to create standardized clips that can be used by all team members. This is particularly useful for maintaining brand voice and ensuring that all external communications are aligned with the company's messaging guidelines.

For instance, customer support teams can use ClipCharm to create a repository of approved responses to common inquiries. This ensures that all team members provide consistent and accurate information, reducing the likelihood of errors and misunderstandings. As a result, customer satisfaction improves, and the team can handle more inquiries efficiently.

Enhanced Collaboration

ClipCharm also fosters better collaboration among team members. By sharing clips, teams can ensure that everyone has access to the same information and resources. This feature is particularly useful for distributed teams or organizations with multiple departments that need to collaborate on projects.

For example, a product development team working on a new software release can use ClipCharm to share technical specifications, user requirements, and other critical information. This ensures that all team members are on the same page and can easily access the information they need to perform their tasks. Additionally, ClipCharm's integration with Microsoft 365 tools like Teams and SharePoint allows for seamless sharing and collaboration, further enhancing productivity.

Reduction of Redundant Work

ClipCharm reduces redundant work by allowing users to reuse existing content. This is particularly beneficial for tasks that require the same information to be used repeatedly. For example, HR departments can create clips for standard onboarding materials, company policies, and training documents. When onboarding a new employee, they can quickly assemble the necessary materials using ClipCharm, rather than recreating the documents from scratch each time.

This not only saves time but also ensures that the information provided to new employees is consistent and up-to-date. Additionally, it allows HR professionals to focus on more strategic tasks, such as improving the onboarding process or developing new training programs.

Improved Knowledge Management

Effective knowledge management is crucial for productivity, and ClipCharm plays a significant role in this area. By creating a centralized repository of clips, organizations can ensure that valuable information is easily accessible to all employees. This reduces the time spent searching for information and minimizes the risk of important knowledge being lost or forgotten.

For example, a sales team can use ClipCharm to store and share clips of successful sales pitches, customer testimonials, and competitive analysis. New sales representatives can quickly get up to speed by reviewing these clips, rather than relying on lengthy training sessions or searching through disparate documents. This accelerates the onboarding process and enables the sales team to be more productive.

Customization and Flexibility

ClipCharm's flexibility allows users to customize their clips to suit their specific needs. This customization can enhance productivity by ensuring that the information used is relevant and tailored to the task at hand. Users can easily modify clips to include the most current data or to address specific requirements, making their work more efficient and effective.

For instance, a project manager can create clips for various project templates, such as status reports, risk assessments, and project plans. These templates can be customized for each project, ensuring that the information is relevant and up-to-date. This not only saves time but also improves the quality of the project documentation.

Integration with Other Tools

ClipCharm's integration with other Microsoft 365 tools further enhances productivity. Users can seamlessly insert clips into Word documents, Excel spreadsheets, PowerPoint presentations, and Outlook emails. This integration ensures that users can leverage the full power of Microsoft 365 while benefiting from the efficiency of ClipCharm.

For example, a financial analyst can use ClipCharm to insert commonly used financial formulas and data analysis templates into Excel spreadsheets. This not only saves time but also ensures accuracy and consistency in the analysis. Similarly, a marketing team can use ClipCharm to quickly assemble PowerPoint presentations with pre-approved slides and graphics, streamlining the presentation creation process.

Conclusion

In conclusion, ClipCharm significantly improves productivity in Microsoft 365 by streamlining workflows, saving time, ensuring consistency and accuracy, enhancing collaboration, reducing redundant work, improving knowledge management, providing customization and flexibility, and integrating seamlessly with other tools. By leveraging these benefits, individuals and teams can work more efficiently, focus on high-value activities, and achieve better results in their daily tasks and projects. ClipCharm is a powerful tool that, when used effectively, can transform the way organizations manage and utilize information, leading to increased productivity and overall success.

1.3.2 Enhanced Collaboration

In the modern workplace, collaboration is paramount. Effective teamwork not only drives productivity but also fosters innovation and ensures that all team members are aligned towards common goals. ClipCharm, as an integral component of Microsoft 365, significantly enhances collaboration in several key ways. This section explores the various ways in which ClipCharm facilitates and improves collaborative efforts within Microsoft 365.

1. Streamlined Communication and Information Sharing

One of the foremost benefits of using ClipCharm in Microsoft 365 is its ability to streamline communication and information sharing. ClipCharm integrates seamlessly with Microsoft 365 applications like Teams, Outlook, and SharePoint, allowing users to share clips, notes, and other critical information effortlessly.

- Microsoft Teams Integration: ClipCharm's integration with Microsoft Teams allows users to share clips directly within team channels and conversations. This feature is particularly useful for teams working on projects that require constant updates and sharing of information. Users can post clips of important data or summaries, making it easy for team members to access and review the information in real-time. The ability to pin and tag clips within Teams ensures that important information is always accessible and organized.

- Outlook Integration: For users who rely heavily on email communication, ClipCharm's integration with Outlook enables the direct insertion of clips into emails. This eliminates the need for attaching multiple documents or lengthy text, streamlining communication by providing concise and relevant information. It also supports the creation of reusable email templates with embedded clips, making it easier to communicate standardized information.

- SharePoint Integration: SharePoint is a powerful tool for document management and collaboration. ClipCharm's integration with SharePoint allows users to embed clips directly into SharePoint sites and libraries. This integration helps in centralizing information and ensuring that all team members have access to the most current data. It also supports version control and collaborative editing of clips, enhancing the overall efficiency of team projects.

2. Real-Time Collaboration and Editing

ClipCharm offers real-time collaboration features that are crucial for teams working on shared projects. These features enable multiple users to work on the same clips simultaneously, making collaborative tasks more efficient and seamless.

- Simultaneous Editing: With ClipCharm, multiple users can edit the same clip at the same time. This real-time editing capability ensures that all changes are instantly visible to all collaborators, reducing the risk of conflicts and inconsistencies. It is particularly useful for teams that need to update data or make revisions collectively.

- Comments and Annotations: ClipCharm provides tools for commenting and annotating clips. Team members can leave feedback, ask questions, or make suggestions directly on the clip, fostering a more interactive and engaging collaborative process. This feature ensures that all feedback is consolidated in one place, making it easier to track and address.

3. Enhanced Project Management

Effective project management relies on the ability to organize and track progress efficiently. ClipCharm contributes to enhanced project management through its organizational and tracking features.

- Task Assignment and Tracking: ClipCharm's features allow users to assign tasks related to specific clips and track their progress. This integration with Microsoft 365's project management tools, such as Planner and Project, ensures that all tasks are managed effectively. Users can set deadlines, assign responsibilities, and monitor the status of tasks, all within the context of the clips they are working on.

- Milestones and Alerts: ClipCharm supports the setting of milestones and alerts associated with clips. This feature helps teams stay on track by notifying them of upcoming deadlines and important milestones. The integration with Microsoft 365's calendar and notification systems ensures that all team members are aware of critical dates and can plan accordingly.

4. Centralized Knowledge Management

Effective collaboration requires easy access to relevant information and knowledge. ClipCharm helps centralize knowledge management by organizing and storing clips in a structured manner.

- Organized Clip Libraries: ClipCharm allows users to create organized libraries of clips, which can be categorized and tagged for easy retrieval. This centralized repository of information ensures that all team members have access to the same set of data and can quickly find the information they need. It also supports version control, allowing teams to track changes and maintain a history of updates.

- Search and Retrieval: The robust search functionality in ClipCharm makes it easy to locate specific clips or information within a large library. Users can search by keywords, tags, or categories, ensuring that they can quickly access the relevant data without sifting through unrelated information. This feature enhances overall efficiency and reduces the time spent searching for information.

5. Improved Transparency and Accountability

Transparency and accountability are essential for effective teamwork. ClipCharm enhances these aspects by providing visibility into collaborative processes and contributions.

- Activity Tracking: ClipCharm tracks user activity and contributions, providing a clear record of who has made changes or updates to a clip. This feature helps in maintaining transparency and accountability, as team members can see who has contributed to or modified specific information. It also aids in identifying areas where additional input or review may be needed.

- Audit Trails: The audit trail feature in ClipCharm provides a detailed history of changes made to clips. This record includes timestamps, user information, and details of modifications, ensuring that all changes are documented and can be reviewed if needed. This level of detail supports accountability and helps in resolving any disputes or questions about the content.

6. Seamless Integration with Workflow Automation

ClipCharm integrates with Microsoft 365's workflow automation tools, such as Power Automate, to streamline and automate repetitive tasks.

- Automated Clip Management: Users can set up automated workflows to manage clips based on specific triggers or conditions. For example, clips can be automatically categorized, tagged, or shared based on predefined rules. This automation reduces the manual effort required for managing clips and ensures consistency in handling information.

- Integration with Business Processes: ClipCharm's integration with workflow automation tools allows users to incorporate clip management into broader business processes. For instance, clips related to project milestones or deliverables can trigger notifications, task assignments, or updates in other Microsoft 365 applications. This seamless integration enhances overall efficiency and ensures that all processes are aligned.

7. Support for Hybrid and Remote Work Environments

In today's hybrid and remote work environments, collaboration tools must support flexible work arrangements. ClipCharm's features are designed to facilitate collaboration regardless of team members' locations.

- Remote Access: ClipCharm is accessible from anywhere, allowing team members to collaborate and access clips from any location. This flexibility supports remote work arrangements and ensures that all team members can stay connected and contribute to projects, regardless of where they are working from.

- Cross-Platform Compatibility: ClipCharm's compatibility with various devices and platforms ensures that users can collaborate effectively whether they are using a desktop, laptop, tablet, or smartphone. This cross-platform support enhances accessibility and ensures that team members can engage with ClipCharm's features no matter what device they are using.

8. Enhanced Security and Compliance

In collaborative environments, security and compliance are critical considerations. ClipCharm integrates with Microsoft 365's security and compliance features to protect sensitive information.

- Data Security: ClipCharm leverages Microsoft 365's security protocols to ensure that clips and related data are protected from unauthorized access. This includes encryption, access controls, and secure authentication methods. Users can be confident that their information is safeguarded against potential threats.

- Compliance Management: ClipCharm supports compliance with industry standards and regulations by providing tools for managing data retention, access controls, and audit trails. This integration helps organizations maintain compliance and adhere to regulatory requirements, ensuring that all collaborative processes meet necessary standards.

Conclusion

ClipCharm's integration with Microsoft 365 offers a wide range of benefits for enhancing collaboration. From streamlining communication and improving real-time editing to supporting project management and ensuring security, ClipCharm provides valuable tools for modern teams. Its seamless integration with Microsoft 365 applications and its ability to support hybrid and remote work environments make it a powerful asset for any organization looking to enhance its collaborative efforts. By leveraging ClipCharm's features, teams can achieve greater efficiency, transparency, and productivity, ultimately driving success in their collaborative endeavors.

CHAPTER II
Getting Started with ClipCharm

2.1 Setting Up ClipCharm

2.1.1 Installing ClipCharm

Introduction

Before you can start using ClipCharm, the first step is to install it on your system. ClipCharm is a powerful tool designed to enhance productivity by integrating seamlessly with Microsoft 365. The installation process is straightforward but varies slightly depending on your operating system and the version of Microsoft 365 you are using. This section will guide you through each step of the installation process, ensuring that ClipCharm is set up correctly and ready to use.

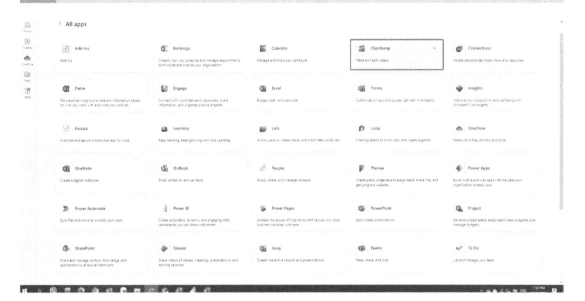

System Requirements

Before starting the installation, it's important to ensure that your system meets the necessary requirements for ClipCharm. These requirements can vary depending on the version of ClipCharm, but generally include:

- Operating System: ClipCharm supports Windows 10 and later versions, as well as macOS 10.14 (Mojave) and later versions. Ensure that your operating system is up to date for the best compatibility.

- Microsoft 365 Subscription: ClipCharm requires an active Microsoft 365 subscription. Make sure you have a valid subscription and are logged into your Microsoft 365 account.

- Internet Connection: A stable internet connection is required for downloading and installing ClipCharm, as well as for accessing updates and online features.

- Disk Space: Ensure you have sufficient disk space for the installation. ClipCharm itself does not require a large amount of space, but additional space may be needed for temporary files and updates.

Downloading ClipCharm

The installation process begins with downloading the ClipCharm installer. Follow these steps to download the latest version of ClipCharm:

1. Visit the Official Website: Go to the ClipCharm official website. If you have a direct link from Microsoft 365, use that link for convenience.

2. Navigate to the Download Section: Look for the 'Downloads' or 'Get ClipCharm' section on the website. This section typically provides links to the installer for different operating systems.

3. Select the Appropriate Version: Choose the version of ClipCharm that matches your operating system. There will generally be separate links for Windows and macOS. Click on the relevant link to start the download.

4. Save the Installer: Save the installer file to a location on your computer where you can easily find it, such as your Desktop or Downloads folder. The file will usually be in `.exe` format for Windows or `.dmg` for macOS.

Installing ClipCharm on Windows

1. Locate the Installer: Navigate to the location where you saved the ClipCharm installer (`.exe` file).

2. Run the Installer: Double-click on the installer file to begin the installation process. If prompted by User Account Control (UAC), click 'Yes' to allow the installer to make changes to your computer.

3. Follow the Installation Wizard: The ClipCharm installation wizard will guide you through the process. Click 'Next' to proceed through the various steps of the installation.

4. Accept the License Agreement: Review the End User License Agreement (EULA) and, if you agree to the terms, select 'I Accept the Agreement' and click 'Next'.

5. Choose the Installation Location: You will be asked to choose the location where ClipCharm will be installed. The default location is usually fine, but you can select a different folder if desired. Click 'Next' to continue.

6. Select Additional Tasks: The installer may give you options for creating shortcuts or associating ClipCharm with certain file types. Choose the options you prefer and click 'Next'.

7. Install ClipCharm: Click 'Install' to begin the installation process. The installer will copy the necessary files to your computer and set up ClipCharm. This may take a few minutes.

8. Complete the Installation: Once the installation is complete, you will see a confirmation screen. Click 'Finish' to close the installer. You may be prompted to restart your computer; if so, save any work and restart as needed.

Installing ClipCharm on macOS

1. Locate the Installer: Open Finder and navigate to the location where you saved the ClipCharm installer (`.dmg` file).

2. Open the Installer: Double-click on the `.dmg` file to mount the ClipCharm installer disk image. A new window will open with the ClipCharm application and a shortcut to your Applications folder.

3. Drag and Drop: Drag the ClipCharm icon into the Applications folder shortcut. This will copy ClipCharm to your Applications folder.

4. Complete the Installation: Once the copying process is complete, you can eject the disk image by right-clicking on it in Finder and selecting 'Eject'. ClipCharm is now installed on your Mac.

5. Open ClipCharm: Navigate to the Applications folder and double-click on ClipCharm to open it. The first time you open ClipCharm, you may receive a warning about opening an application downloaded from the internet. Confirm that you want to open the application.

Setting Up ClipCharm

Once ClipCharm is installed, the next step is to configure it for use with Microsoft 365:

1. Launch ClipCharm: Open ClipCharm from your applications menu or desktop shortcut.

2. Sign In: You will be prompted to sign in with your Microsoft 365 account. Enter your credentials and click 'Sign In'. This will connect ClipCharm with your Microsoft 365 subscription.

3. Grant Permissions: ClipCharm may require certain permissions to function properly, such as access to your files and Microsoft 365 apps. Review and grant the necessary permissions to ensure full functionality.

4. Configure Settings: Navigate to the settings or preferences menu within ClipCharm to customize your setup. You can configure options such as default save locations, integration settings with Microsoft 365 apps, and user interface preferences.

5. Update ClipCharm: Check for any available updates for ClipCharm and install them if necessary. Keeping ClipCharm up to date ensures you have access to the latest features and bug fixes.

Testing the Installation

After completing the installation and initial setup, it's a good idea to test ClipCharm to ensure everything is working correctly:

1. Create a Test Clip: Open ClipCharm and create a test clip to verify that the basic functionality is working. Follow the instructions in the next section of this guide for creating and managing clips.

2. Verify Integration: Check the integration with Microsoft 365 apps by opening a document in Word or Excel and using ClipCharm to add or manage clips.

3. Check for Issues: If you encounter any issues, consult the troubleshooting section of this guide or visit the ClipCharm support website for assistance.

Troubleshooting Installation Issues

If you encounter problems during the installation of ClipCharm, consider the following solutions:

- Check System Requirements: Ensure that your system meets the minimum requirements for ClipCharm and that your operating system is up to date.

- Verify Internet Connection: A stable internet connection is required for downloading and installing ClipCharm. Check your connection and try again if necessary.

- Reinstall ClipCharm: If the installation fails or you encounter errors, try uninstalling and then reinstalling ClipCharm. Follow the instructions provided earlier for uninstalling ClipCharm if needed.

- Consult Support: If you continue to experience issues, consult the ClipCharm support website or contact customer support for assistance.

Conclusion

Installing ClipCharm is a straightforward process that sets the stage for leveraging its powerful features within Microsoft 365. By following the steps outlined in this section, you can ensure that ClipCharm is correctly installed and ready to enhance your productivity. In the next section, you will learn how to navigate the ClipCharm interface and familiarize yourself with its key sections and features.

2.1.2 Initial Configuration

Once ClipCharm is successfully installed on your Microsoft 365 environment, the next critical step is configuring the application to fit your specific needs. Initial configuration ensures that ClipCharm is tailored to your preferences and workflow, allowing you to maximize its potential from the get-go. This section will guide you through the essential configuration steps, covering user settings, interface customization, and integration with other Microsoft 365 tools.

User Settings

The first aspect of initial configuration involves setting up user preferences. These settings will influence how ClipCharm behaves and interacts with your content. Follow these steps to configure your user settings:

1. Accessing User Settings:

   - Open ClipCharm from your Microsoft 365 dashboard.

   - Navigate to the settings icon, usually represented by a gear symbol, located in the top-right corner of the ClipCharm interface.

   - Click on the settings icon to open the user settings menu.

2. Profile Configuration:

- In the user settings menu, click on "Profile."

- Enter your personal information such as name, email address, and profile picture. This information will help personalize your ClipCharm experience and facilitate collaboration with other users.

3. Language and Region:

- Under the "General" tab, select your preferred language from the dropdown menu. ClipCharm supports multiple languages to cater to a diverse user base.

- Set your time zone to ensure that all time-stamped activities, such as clip creation and updates, are accurately recorded.

4. Notification Preferences:

- Navigate to the "Notifications" tab.

- Customize your notification settings based on your preferences. You can choose to receive notifications via email, in-app alerts, or push notifications for various activities such as clip updates, collaboration invites, and system announcements.

5. Security Settings:

- In the "Security" tab, configure your security settings to protect your data and ensure privacy.

- Set up two-factor authentication (2FA) for an added layer of security. This involves linking your ClipCharm account to your mobile device or email for verification purposes.

Interface Customization

ClipCharm allows you to customize its interface to better align with your workflow and aesthetic preferences. Personalizing the interface can enhance your user experience and make navigation more intuitive. Follow these steps to customize the ClipCharm interface:

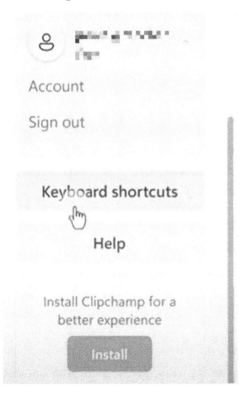

1. *Theme Selection:*

- In the settings menu, go to the "Appearance" tab.

- Choose a theme that suits your preference. ClipCharm offers various themes, including light, dark, and high-contrast options, to accommodate different visual needs and reduce eye strain.

2. *Layout Configuration:*

- Still in the "Appearance" tab, configure the layout settings. You can adjust the positioning of toolbars, side panels, and clip previews to create a workspace that feels comfortable and efficient.

- Enable or disable specific interface elements based on your usage patterns. For instance, you might choose to hide the navigation bar if you prefer a minimalist workspace.

3. *Keyboard Shortcuts:*

- Customize keyboard shortcuts to speed up your workflow. In the "Shortcuts" tab, you can view existing shortcuts and modify them to your liking.

- Create new shortcuts for frequently used actions such as creating a new clip, saving changes, or accessing the clip library.

4. Widgets and Plugins:

- ClipCharm supports various widgets and plugins that can be added to your interface for additional functionality.

- Navigate to the "Plugins" tab in the settings menu and browse the available options. Popular plugins include productivity trackers, content calendars, and integration tools for other Microsoft 365 applications.

Integration with Microsoft 365 Tools

One of ClipCharm's most powerful features is its seamless integration with other Microsoft 365 tools. This integration enhances collaboration and ensures a cohesive workflow across different applications. To set up these integrations, follow these steps:

1. Connecting to Microsoft OneDrive:

- In the settings menu, select the "Integrations" tab.

- Click on "Connect" next to the OneDrive option.

- Authenticate your Microsoft account to grant ClipCharm access to your OneDrive storage. This allows you to save and retrieve clips directly from your cloud storage.

2. Syncing with Microsoft Teams:

- In the "Integrations" tab, find the Microsoft Teams option and click "Connect."

- Authorize ClipCharm to access your Teams account. Once connected, you can share clips within Teams channels, initiate discussions about specific clips, and collaborate in real-time with your team members.

3. Linking with Microsoft Outlook:

- To integrate ClipCharm with Outlook, navigate to the "Integrations" tab and select "Connect" next to Outlook.

- Grant ClipCharm permission to access your Outlook account. This integration allows you to attach clips to emails, set reminders for clip-related tasks, and schedule clip updates using your Outlook calendar.

4. Utilizing Microsoft SharePoint:

- In the same "Integrations" tab, click on "Connect" next to SharePoint.

- Authenticate your SharePoint account to enable ClipCharm to interact with your SharePoint sites. You can then embed clips in SharePoint pages, share clips across different sites, and manage clip permissions through SharePoint.

Setting Up Templates

Templates in ClipCharm can save you significant time and effort by providing pre-defined structures for your clips. Setting up templates involves creating and configuring them to match your typical content requirements. Here's how to do it:

1. Accessing the Template Library:

- Open ClipCharm and navigate to the "Templates" section from the main menu.

- Browse through the available templates. ClipCharm offers a variety of default templates suited for different purposes such as meeting notes, project updates, and content drafts.

2. Creating Custom Templates:

- Click on "Create New Template" to start designing your custom template.

- Define the structure and layout of your template. Add sections, headers, placeholders, and formatting styles that you frequently use in your clips.

- Save your custom template with a descriptive name to easily identify it later.

3. Configuring Template Settings:

  - In the "Template Settings" menu, specify the default options for your template. This includes setting default fonts, colors, and element sizes.

  - Determine the access permissions for your template. You can choose to keep it private, share it with specific team members, or make it publicly available within your organization.

4. Using Templates:

  - To use a template, navigate to the "Create Clip" menu and select "From Template."

  - Choose your desired template from the list and start populating it with your content. Templates ensure consistency and help maintain a professional look across all your clips.

Finalizing Initial Configuration

After setting up user settings, customizing the interface, integrating with other Microsoft 365 tools, and configuring templates, it's essential to finalize your initial configuration. This involves reviewing your settings to ensure everything is correctly set up and ready for efficient use.

1. Review and Adjust Settings:

  - Go through each section of the settings menu once more to verify that all configurations are to your liking.

  - Make any necessary adjustments based on your review. Ensure that all integrations are correctly authorized and functioning.

2. Test the Configuration:

  - Create a few test clips to ensure that your settings and customizations are working as expected.

  - Test the integration features by sharing clips via Microsoft Teams, attaching clips in Outlook, and saving clips to OneDrive.

3. Backup Your Configuration:

  - In the "Backup" tab of the settings menu, create a backup of your configuration settings. This ensures that you can restore your setup in case of any issues or when migrating to a new device.

- Schedule regular backups to keep your configuration data safe.

4. Seek Feedback:

- If you're part of a team, share your configuration setup with colleagues and seek feedback.

- Make adjustments based on their suggestions to improve the overall user experience.

By following these detailed steps for initial configuration, you can ensure that ClipCharm is optimized for your needs right from the start. Proper configuration not only enhances your productivity but also ensures a smooth and efficient workflow within the Microsoft 365 environment.

2.2 Navigating the ClipCharm Interface

2.2.1 Dashboard Overview

Navigating the ClipCharm interface is essential for effectively utilizing its features and maximizing productivity. The dashboard serves as the central hub for all activities within ClipCharm, providing a comprehensive view of your projects, clips, and settings. This section will guide you through the key components of the dashboard, offering detailed explanations and tips for efficient navigation and use.

Introduction to the Dashboard

The ClipCharm dashboard is designed to be user-friendly and intuitive, allowing users to quickly access and manage their clips and projects. Upon logging in, you will be greeted by the main dashboard screen, which is divided into several sections, each serving a specific purpose.

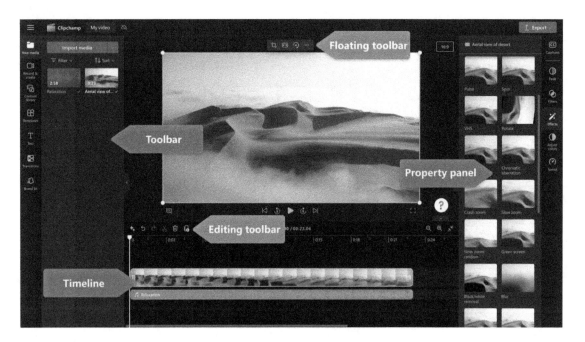

Main Sections of the Dashboard

1. Navigation Bar

The navigation bar is typically located at the top of the dashboard. It contains various menus and icons that provide quick access to different parts of ClipCharm. Key elements of the navigation bar include:

- Home Icon: Takes you back to the main dashboard screen from any other section.

- Clips Library: Access your collection of clips, categorized and searchable for easy retrieval.

- Projects: Manage and organize your ongoing projects, with options to create new projects or view existing ones.

- Templates: Browse and use pre-designed templates to streamline your clip creation process.

- Settings: Customize your ClipCharm settings, including user preferences, account details, and notification settings.

- Help: Access support resources, tutorials, and contact options for technical assistance.

2. Sidebar Menu

The sidebar menu, usually located on the left side of the screen, provides additional navigation options and quick access to specific features. The sidebar menu typically includes:

- Dashboard Overview: A summary of your recent activity, including recently accessed clips and projects.

- Favorites: Quick access to clips and projects you have marked as favorites.

- Recent Activity: A log of your recent actions, such as clips created, edited, or shared.

- Notifications: Alerts and updates about your projects, shared clips, and other important information.

3. Main Workspace

The main workspace occupies the central area of the dashboard. It displays detailed information and options based on the section you are currently viewing. For example, if you are in the Clips Library, the main workspace will show your clips organized by categories, with options to search, filter, and sort them. If you are managing a project, the main workspace will display project details, timelines, and collaboration options.

4. Search Bar

The search bar is a powerful tool located at the top of the main workspace. It allows you to quickly find clips, projects, templates, and other resources within ClipCharm. The search bar supports various filters and sorting options to help you narrow down your results and find exactly what you need.

5. Quick Action Buttons

Quick action buttons are strategically placed throughout the dashboard to provide easy access to frequently used functions. These buttons may include:

- Create New Clip: Start a new clip creation process with a single click.

- Upload Clip: Upload an existing clip from your device to your ClipCharm library.

- Share Clip: Quickly share a clip with team members or external collaborators.

- Edit Clip: Open a clip in the editor for modifications and enhancements.

Navigating the Dashboard: Step-by-Step

To help you become familiar with the ClipCharm dashboard, here is a step-by-step guide to navigating its main sections:

Step 1: Logging In

When you first log in to ClipCharm, you will be directed to the main dashboard screen. Take a moment to familiarize yourself with the layout and the key sections described above.

Step 2: Exploring the Navigation Bar

Hover over each icon in the navigation bar to see tooltips that describe their function. Click on each icon to explore the different sections of ClipCharm, such as the Clips Library, Projects, and Templates.

Step 3: Using the Sidebar Menu

Open the sidebar menu by clicking on the menu icon (usually represented by three horizontal lines). Browse through the available options, such as Dashboard Overview, Favorites, and Recent Activity. Click on each option to view the corresponding content in the main workspace.

Step 4: Accessing the Main Workspace

The main workspace is where you will spend most of your time in ClipCharm. Depending on the section you are viewing, the main workspace will display different content and options. For example, if you are in the Clips Library, you will see a list of your clips, along with search and filter options.

Step 5: Utilizing the Search Bar

Type keywords into the search bar to find specific clips, projects, or templates. Use the available filters and sorting options to refine your search results. The search bar is a powerful tool that can save you time and help you quickly locate the resources you need.

Step 6: Performing Quick Actions

Look for quick action buttons throughout the dashboard. These buttons allow you to perform common tasks, such as creating new clips, uploading existing clips, sharing clips, and editing clips. Click on these buttons to initiate the corresponding actions.

Tips for Efficient Dashboard Navigation

To make the most of the ClipCharm dashboard, consider the following tips:

- Customize Your Sidebar Menu: Adjust the sidebar menu to display the options you use most frequently. This can help you access important features more quickly.

- Use Favorites: Mark frequently accessed clips and projects as favorites to easily find them in the Favorites section.

- Stay Organized: Regularly organize your clips and projects into categories and folders to keep your library manageable and easy to navigate.

- Leverage the Search Bar: Use the search bar often to quickly locate clips and projects, especially as your library grows.

- Take Advantage of Templates: Use pre-designed templates to streamline your clip creation process and maintain consistency across your projects.

Conclusion

The ClipCharm dashboard is designed to provide a seamless and efficient user experience. By familiarizing yourself with its layout and features, you can navigate ClipCharm with ease and maximize your productivity. Whether you are creating new clips, managing projects, or collaborating with team members, the dashboard serves as your central hub for all activities within ClipCharm. Take the time to explore and customize the dashboard to suit your workflow, and you will find that ClipCharm becomes an invaluable tool in your Microsoft 365 toolkit.

2.2.2 Key Sections and Features

The ClipCharm interface is designed to be intuitive and user-friendly, providing a seamless experience for creating, managing, and sharing clips. The key sections and features include the Dashboard, Clip Library, Clip Editor, Templates, and Settings. Each of these sections offers specific functionalities that streamline your workflow and enhance productivity.

Dashboard

The Dashboard serves as the central hub of ClipCharm, providing an overview of your recent activities, upcoming tasks, and quick access to key features. When you first log in to ClipCharm, the Dashboard is the first thing you see. It is designed to give you a snapshot of your current projects and to help you navigate to other sections quickly.

- Recent Clips: This area displays the clips you have recently created or edited. It allows you to quickly access and continue working on them without having to search through your Clip Library.

- Upcoming Tasks: Here, you can see a list of tasks or deadlines related to your clip projects. This feature helps you stay organized and ensures you meet your deadlines.

- Quick Access Toolbar: The toolbar provides shortcuts to frequently used features such as creating a new clip, accessing templates, and viewing your Clip Library.

Clip Library

The Clip Library is where all your clips are stored. It offers powerful organizational tools that make it easy to manage and retrieve your clips whenever needed.

- Folders and Subfolders: You can organize your clips into folders and subfolders, much like a file system on your computer. This hierarchical structure allows you to group related clips together for easy access.

- Search and Filter: The search bar at the top of the Clip Library allows you to quickly find specific clips by name or keywords. Additionally, you can use filters to narrow down your search results based on criteria such as creation date, tags, or author.

- Tags and Categories: You can assign tags and categories to your clips to further organize them. Tags are keywords that describe the content of your clip, making it easier to search and filter. Categories are broader groups that can encompass multiple tags.

Clip Editor

The Clip Editor is the core feature of ClipCharm, where you create and modify your clips. It provides a rich set of tools and functionalities to help you produce high-quality clips efficiently.

- Editing Tools: The Clip Editor offers a variety of editing tools, including text formatting, image insertion, and video trimming. These tools allow you to customize your clips to meet your specific needs.

- Preview Pane: The preview pane gives you a real-time view of how your clip will look once published. This feature is invaluable for ensuring that your clip meets your expectations before finalizing it.

- Undo and Redo: These essential tools allow you to easily revert or reapply changes, giving you the flexibility to experiment with different edits without fear of making irreversible mistakes.

Templates

Templates are pre-designed clip layouts that you can use to streamline the creation process. ClipCharm offers a wide range of templates for various purposes, including marketing materials, educational content, and internal communications.

- Template Library: The Template Library contains a collection of pre-made templates that you can browse and select from. These templates are categorized by use case, making it easy to find one that suits your needs.

- Custom Templates: In addition to the built-in templates, you can create and save your own custom templates. This feature is particularly useful if you frequently create clips with a similar structure or design.

- Template Editor: The Template Editor allows you to modify existing templates or create new ones from scratch. You can adjust the layout, add or remove elements, and customize the design to match your brand guidelines.

Settings

The Settings section allows you to customize ClipCharm to better suit your workflow and preferences. It includes options for personalizing your user experience, managing account settings, and configuring integrations with other Microsoft 365 tools.

- User Preferences: Here, you can adjust various aspects of the ClipCharm interface, such as theme (light or dark mode), language, and notification preferences.

- Account Management: This area lets you update your account information, change your password, and manage your subscription.

- Integrations: ClipCharm can be integrated with other Microsoft 365 applications, such as Outlook, Teams, and SharePoint. This section allows you to configure and manage these integrations to ensure seamless interoperability between ClipCharm and the rest of your Microsoft 365 ecosystem.

Collaboration Features

Collaboration is a key aspect of ClipCharm, enabling multiple users to work together on clip projects efficiently. The interface includes several features designed to facilitate teamwork and communication.

- Sharing Options: You can share clips with team members or external collaborators via email, link, or directly within Microsoft Teams. Sharing settings allow you to control access permissions, ensuring that only authorized users can view or edit your clips.

- Comments and Feedback: The commenting feature allows collaborators to leave feedback directly on the clip. This real-time communication helps streamline the review and approval process.

- Version History: ClipCharm maintains a version history for each clip, allowing you to track changes and revert to previous versions if needed. This feature is particularly useful in collaborative environments where multiple users may be making edits.

Help and Support

ClipCharm provides extensive help and support resources to assist you in using the tool effectively. These resources are accessible directly from the interface, ensuring you have the information you need at your fingertips.

- Help Center: The Help Center contains a comprehensive collection of articles, tutorials, and FAQs that cover all aspects of using ClipCharm. You can search for specific topics or browse through the categories to find the information you need.

- Live Chat Support: For immediate assistance, ClipCharm offers live chat support with knowledgeable representatives who can help you resolve issues in real-time.

- User Community: The user community is a forum where you can connect with other ClipCharm users to share tips, ask questions, and discuss best practices. This collaborative environment fosters knowledge sharing and provides additional support from your peers.

Mobile Access

In today's mobile-first world, having access to ClipCharm on your mobile devices is essential. The mobile version of ClipCharm offers many of the same features as the desktop version, allowing you to create, edit, and manage clips on the go.

- Mobile Interface: The mobile interface is optimized for touchscreens, providing a seamless user experience on smartphones and tablets. The layout is simplified to ensure easy navigation and functionality on smaller screens.

- Syncing and Access: Your clips are automatically synced across all your devices, ensuring that you have access to your latest work no matter where you are. You can start a clip on your desktop and continue editing it on your mobile device without missing a beat.

- Notifications: The mobile app can send push notifications to keep you informed of important updates, such as new comments on your clips or approaching deadlines. This feature helps you stay connected and responsive, even when you are away from your computer.

Security Features

Security is a top priority for ClipCharm, especially when dealing with sensitive or proprietary content. The interface includes several features designed to protect your data and ensure secure access to your clips.

- Encryption: All data transmitted between your device and ClipCharm servers is encrypted using industry-standard protocols. This ensures that your clips and personal information are protected from unauthorized access.

- Access Controls: You can set granular access controls for each clip, specifying who can view, edit, or share it. This feature helps you maintain control over your content and ensures that only authorized users can make changes.

- Audit Logs: ClipCharm maintains an audit log of all actions taken within the tool, providing a detailed record of who did what and when. This log can be useful for tracking changes, identifying potential security issues, and ensuring compliance with organizational policies.

Reporting and Analytics

Understanding how your clips are being used and their impact is crucial for continuous improvement. ClipCharm offers robust reporting and analytics features that provide insights into your clip usage and performance.

- Usage Reports: These reports give you an overview of how your clips are being used, including metrics such as view counts, shares, and engagement rates. This information can help you identify which clips are most effective and where there may be opportunities for improvement.

- Engagement Analytics: Engagement analytics provide deeper insights into how viewers are interacting with your clips. You can see which parts of the clip are most engaging, where viewers are dropping off, and how long they are spending on each section.

- Custom Reports: ClipCharm allows you to create custom reports tailored to your specific needs. You can choose the metrics you want to track, set up automated reporting schedules, and export the data for further analysis.

Conclusion

Navigating the ClipCharm interface and understanding its key sections and features are fundamental steps in mastering this powerful tool. By familiarizing yourself with the Dashboard, Clip Library, Clip Editor, Templates, Settings, Collaboration Features, Help and Support, Mobile Access, Security Features, and Reporting and Analytics, you can fully leverage ClipCharm to enhance your productivity and streamline your workflow within Microsoft 365. Whether you are creating clips for marketing, education, or internal communication, ClipCharm provides the tools and functionalities you need to succeed.

2.3 Understanding Basic Functions

2.3.1 Creating and Managing Clips

Creating and managing clips in ClipCharm is a fundamental skill that enables users to efficiently capture, store, and utilize various pieces of information. This section will walk you through the step-by-step process of creating and managing clips, ensuring you can take full advantage of ClipCharm's capabilities.

Creating Clips

Creating clips is the primary function of ClipCharm, allowing users to capture snippets of information from various sources. Here's how you can create clips in ClipCharm:

Step-by-Step Guide to Creating Clips

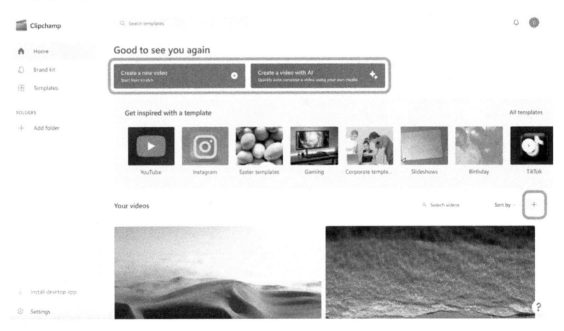

1. Open ClipCharm:

   - Launch ClipCharm from your Microsoft 365 dashboard or start menu.

- Ensure you are logged in with your Microsoft 365 account to access all features.

2. Access the Clip Creation Tool:

   - Navigate to the main dashboard.

   - Click on the "Create Clip" button prominently displayed on the interface.

3. Select Source of Content:

   - You can create clips from various sources including text documents, web pages, emails, or any on-screen content.

   - Choose the source by either pasting the content, uploading a file, or using the integrated web clipper.

4. Highlight and Clip Content:

   - Use your mouse to highlight the text or content you wish to clip.

   - Click the "Clip" button that appears once you have selected the content.

5. Annotate and Tag Clips:

   - After clipping, a window will pop up allowing you to add notes, tags, and categories to your clip.

   - Use descriptive tags and categories to make your clips easily searchable later.

6. Save the Clip:

   - Click "Save" to store the clip in your ClipCharm library.

   - Your clip is now available for future reference and can be accessed anytime.

Creating Clips from Different Sources

- Text Documents:

   - Open the document within ClipCharm or use the ClipCharm add-in for Word.

   - Highlight the desired text and clip it following the steps above.

- Web Pages:

- Use the ClipCharm browser extension to clip content directly from web pages.

- Navigate to the web page, highlight the text, and click the ClipCharm icon.

- Emails:

  - Open the email in Outlook or another email client.

  - Highlight the important information and use the ClipCharm integration to create a clip.

Managing Clips

Effective clip management ensures that your clips remain organized, easily accessible, and useful. ClipCharm provides several features to help you manage your clips efficiently.

Organizing Clips

1. Categorizing Clips:

   - Use categories to group related clips together.

   - Create categories based on projects, subjects, or any organizational scheme that suits your workflow.

2. Tagging Clips:

   - Tags are keywords that describe the content of the clip.

   - Use multiple tags for each clip to enhance searchability.

3. Using Folders:

   - Create folders within ClipCharm to store and organize clips.

   - Move clips into folders by dragging and dropping or using the "Move to Folder" option.

Searching for Clips

1. Search Bar:

   - Use the search bar at the top of the ClipCharm interface to find clips quickly.

   - Enter keywords, tags, or categories to locate specific clips.

2. Advanced Search Filters:

  - Apply filters such as date created, source type, or tags to narrow down search results.

  - Combine multiple filters for more precise searching.

Editing and Updating Clips

1. Accessing Clip Details:

  - Click on a clip to view its details, including the source, notes, and tags.

  - Use the edit option to make changes to the clip content or metadata.

2. Updating Content:

  - If the source content has changed, update the clip by re-clipping the new content.

  - Ensure that the clip reflects the most current information.

3. Adding Notes and Annotations:

  - Add additional notes or annotations to clips as needed.

  - Use these notes to provide context or additional information that may be useful later.

Deleting and Restoring Clips

1. Deleting Clips:

  - To delete a clip, select it and click the "Delete" button.

  - Confirm the deletion when prompted to remove the clip from your library.

2. Restoring Deleted Clips:

  - Deleted clips are moved to the "Recycle Bin" where they can be restored.

  - Access the Recycle Bin from the ClipCharm dashboard and restore clips if needed.

Sharing Clips

1. Sharing with Team Members:

   - Select the clip you wish to share and click the "Share" button.

   - Choose team members from your contact list and send the clip directly to them.

2. Collaborative Editing:

   - Shared clips can be edited collaboratively.

   - Changes made by any team member are reflected in real-time.

3. Setting Permissions:

   - Set permissions for each shared clip, such as view-only or edit access.

   - Control who can see or modify the clip.

Best Practices for Clip Management

1. Regular Maintenance:

   - Periodically review your clip library to remove outdated or irrelevant clips.

   - Keep your library organized by regularly updating categories and tags.

2. Consistent Tagging:

   - Develop a consistent tagging system to make searching more efficient.

   - Use specific and descriptive tags for better organization.

3. Backup and Export:

   - Regularly back up your clips to avoid data loss.

   - Use the export feature to save clips in different formats or move them to other platforms.

4. Collaborative Workflows:

   - Encourage team members to use consistent categories and tags.

   - Establish clear guidelines for collaborative editing and sharing.

By mastering the creation and management of clips in ClipCharm, you can significantly enhance your productivity and organization within Microsoft 365. These skills will enable you to capture essential information efficiently, keep your clips well-organized, and easily share them with others, making ClipCharm an indispensable tool in your daily workflow.

2.3.2 Using Templates

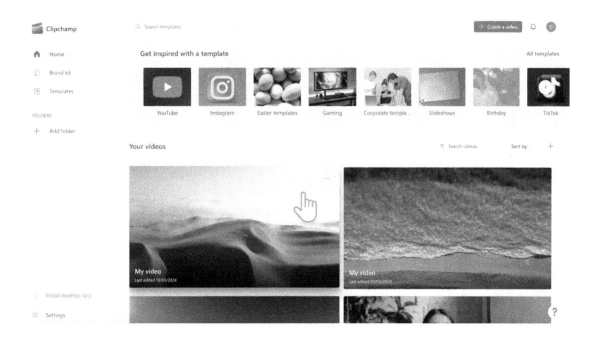

Using templates in ClipCharm is a powerful way to streamline your workflow, maintain consistency, and enhance productivity. Templates allow you to create a predefined structure for your clips, ensuring that all essential elements are included every time. This section will guide you through the process of using templates in ClipCharm, from understanding their benefits to creating and customizing your own templates.

Benefits of Using Templates

1. Consistency: Templates ensure that all your clips follow a uniform structure, making them easier to read and understand. This is particularly important in a collaborative environment where multiple users contribute to the clip library.

2. Efficiency: Templates save time by providing a ready-made format that you can quickly fill in with specific content. This reduces the need to start from scratch for each new clip, allowing you to focus more on content quality rather than formatting.

3. Professionalism: Using templates helps maintain a professional appearance across all your clips. This is crucial when sharing clips with clients, stakeholders, or team members, as it reflects a well-organized and methodical approach.

Types of Templates

ClipCharm offers various types of templates to cater to different needs:

1. Text Templates: These templates provide a structure for text-based clips. They can include headings, subheadings, bullet points, and placeholder text to guide the content creation process.

2. Multimedia Templates: Designed for clips that include images, videos, or audio, these templates help organize multimedia content alongside text descriptions and captions.

3. Project Templates: For comprehensive projects, these templates offer a framework that includes multiple sections, each with its own set of guidelines and placeholders. This is ideal for larger clips that require detailed planning and organization.

Creating a Template

To create a template in ClipCharm, follow these steps:

1. Access the Template Library: Open ClipCharm and navigate to the Template Library. This is typically found in the main menu or dashboard.

2. Select 'Create New Template': Click on the option to create a new template. This will open a blank template editor.

3. Define the Structure: Start by defining the basic structure of your template. Add headings, subheadings, and placeholders for text, images, videos, or other content types.

You can also include instructions or guidelines for each section to assist users in filling out the template correctly.

4. Customize Formatting: Customize the formatting of your template to match your style preferences. Adjust font sizes, colors, and alignment to ensure that the template is visually appealing and easy to read.

5. Save the Template: Once you are satisfied with the structure and formatting, save the template to your Template Library. Give it a descriptive name that indicates its purpose, making it easy to identify and reuse in the future.

Using a Template

To use a template for creating a new clip, follow these steps:

1. Choose a Template: Open ClipCharm and navigate to the Template Library. Browse through the available templates and select the one that best fits your needs.

2. Open the Template: Click on the chosen template to open it in the clip editor. The predefined structure will be loaded, ready for you to fill in with specific content.

3. Fill in the Content: Start filling in the content according to the placeholders and guidelines provided in the template. For text templates, replace the placeholder text with your own. For multimedia templates, upload images, videos, or audio files to the designated sections.

4. Customize as Needed: While templates provide a predefined structure, you can still customize them to suit your specific requirements. Add or remove sections, adjust formatting, and make any necessary changes to ensure the clip meets your needs.

5. Save and Publish: Once you have filled in the content and customized the template, save the clip. You can then publish it to your Clip Library or share it with team members or other stakeholders.

Best Practices for Using Templates

1. Start Simple: When creating templates, start with a simple structure that can be easily understood and followed. As you become more comfortable with the template creation process, you can add more complexity and detail.

2. Include Clear Instructions: Ensure that your templates include clear instructions or guidelines for each section. This helps users understand what content is expected and how to fill out the template correctly.

3. Use Consistent Formatting: Maintain consistent formatting across all templates to create a cohesive look and feel. This includes using the same font styles, colors, and alignment for headings, subheadings, and body text.

4. Regularly Update Templates: Review and update your templates regularly to ensure they remain relevant and useful. This is particularly important if there are changes in your content strategy, branding guidelines, or ClipCharm features.

5. Encourage Feedback: Encourage team members to provide feedback on the templates they use. This can help identify areas for improvement and ensure that the templates meet the needs of all users.

Conclusion

Using templates in ClipCharm is an effective way to enhance productivity, maintain consistency, and ensure professionalism in your content creation process. By understanding the benefits of templates, learning how to create and use them, and following best practices, you can significantly improve your workflow and collaboration within Microsoft 365. Whether you are working on text-based clips, multimedia projects, or comprehensive content plans, templates provide a valuable framework to streamline your efforts and achieve better results.

CHAPTER III
Using ClipCharm for Content Creation

3.1 Creating Clips

Creating clips in ClipCharm is a fundamental task that enables users to harness the full potential of this powerful tool within the Microsoft 365 ecosystem. This section provides a comprehensive guide to creating clips, including a detailed step-by-step process to ensure you can quickly and efficiently generate the content you need.

3.1.1 Step-by-Step Guide to Creating Clips

Introduction to Clips:

Before diving into the creation process, it's essential to understand what clips are. Clips in ClipCharm are small, manageable segments of content that can be easily edited, organized, and integrated into larger projects. They can include text, images, videos, and other multimedia elements, making them versatile for various use cases, from presentations to reports.

Step 1: Accessing the ClipCharm Interface

1. Open Microsoft 365: Start by opening your Microsoft 365 application. ClipCharm can be accessed from various Microsoft 365 tools such as Word, Excel, and PowerPoint.

2. Navigate to ClipCharm: Locate the ClipCharm icon in the toolbar. Clicking this will open the ClipCharm dashboard, where you can manage and create your clips.

Step 2: Creating a New Clip

1. Initiate a New Clip: In the ClipCharm dashboard, find and click the 'New Clip' button. This will open a new window or pane where you can start creating your clip.

2. Choose the Clip Type: Depending on your content needs, select the type of clip you want to create. Options typically include text, image, video, and mixed media clips. For this guide, we will create a text-based clip.

Step 3: Entering Content

1. Title Your Clip: Begin by giving your clip a title. This should be descriptive enough to easily identify the clip later.

2. Add Content: In the main content area, start typing or paste the text you want to include in your clip. You can also insert images, links, and other multimedia elements using the toolbar options.

3. Formatting Text: Use the formatting tools to style your text. This includes options for bold, italic, underline, font size, and color. Proper formatting ensures your clip is both visually appealing and easy to read.

Step 4: Customizing Your Clip

1. Add Tags and Categories: To help organize your clips, add relevant tags and categorize them. This makes it easier to search and filter clips later.

2. Set Permissions: If you plan to share this clip with others, set the appropriate permissions. You can choose who can view, edit, or comment on your clip.

3. Insert Media: If your clip requires images or videos, use the insert function to upload or link to the necessary media. Ensure these elements are well-integrated into your text for a cohesive presentation.

Step 5: Reviewing and Editing

1. Review Content: Before finalizing your clip, thoroughly review the content for any errors or necessary adjustments.

2. Edit as Needed: Make any necessary edits to improve clarity, fix typos, or enhance the overall quality of your clip.

3. Preview Clip: Use the preview function to see how your clip will appear when shared or integrated into other documents.

Step 6: Saving and Publishing

1. Save Your Clip: Once satisfied with your clip, save it. ClipCharm typically has an autosave feature, but it's good practice to manually save as well.

2. Publish or Share: If your clip is ready for others, publish it to your ClipCharm library or share it directly with team members or collaborators.

Step 7: Using Your Clip

1. Insert into Documents: With your clip created, you can now insert it into other Microsoft 365 documents. Simply drag and drop the clip from your ClipCharm library into your Word, Excel, or PowerPoint file.

2. Reuse and Repurpose: One of the significant advantages of ClipCharm is the ability to reuse clips. You can repurpose your clip in multiple projects without needing to recreate content from scratch.

Tips for Effective Clip Creation:

1. Be Concise: Keep clips focused and to the point. Avoid unnecessary information that can clutter your content.

2. Use High-Quality Media: Ensure any images or videos included are high quality to maintain a professional appearance.

3. Consistent Formatting: Maintain consistency in formatting to create a unified look across all your clips.

4. Regular Updates: Periodically review and update your clips to ensure they remain current and relevant.

Common Mistakes to Avoid:

1. Overloading Clips: Avoid stuffing too much information into a single clip. If needed, create multiple clips for different sections or topics.

2. Neglecting Tags: Proper tagging is crucial for organization. Don't skip this step, as it greatly enhances searchability.

3. Ignoring Permissions: Always set the correct permissions to control who can access and modify your clips.

Conclusion:

Creating clips in ClipCharm is a straightforward process that, when done correctly, can significantly enhance your productivity and content management within Microsoft 365. By following this step-by-step guide, you can efficiently create, customize, and utilize clips to streamline your workflow and improve collaboration with your team. Whether you're creating simple text snippets or complex multimedia presentations, ClipCharm provides the tools you need to organize and optimize your content creation efforts.

3.1.2 Editing and Customizing Clips

Editing and customizing clips is a critical aspect of utilizing ClipCharm effectively. Once you have created your initial clips, enhancing them to fit your specific needs and preferences is essential for maximizing their utility. This section will guide you through the various tools and techniques available in ClipCharm for editing and customizing your clips, ensuring they meet your exact requirements.

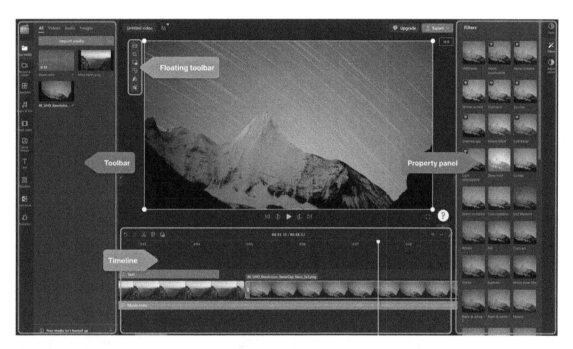

Understanding ClipCharm's Editing Interface

Before diving into the specifics of editing and customizing clips, it's important to familiarize yourself with ClipCharm's editing interface. The editing tools are designed to provide a seamless experience, allowing you to make adjustments quickly and efficiently.

1. Accessing the Editing Interface

 - To edit a clip, start by locating the clip you want to modify within your Clip Library. Click on the clip to open it. Once opened, you'll see an "Edit" button or an icon representing editing options.

- Clicking this will take you to the editing interface, where you'll have access to various tools and options for modifying the clip.

2. Editing Tools Overview

- Text Editor: Modify text content within your clip, including font styles, sizes, colors, and alignment.

- Image Editor: Adjust images within the clip, including cropping, resizing, and applying filters.

- Audio Editor: Edit audio tracks if your clip includes sound. This might involve trimming, volume adjustment, or adding effects.

- Video Editor: If working with video clips, you can cut, trim, and merge video segments, adjust playback speed, and add visual effects.

Text Editing and Customization

Text is a fundamental component of many clips, and ClipCharm provides robust tools for text editing and customization. Here's how to make the most of these features:

1. Editing Text Content

- Select the Text: Click on the text you wish to edit. You'll be able to type directly into the text box to make changes.

- Font Customization: Adjust font type, size, weight, and style. ClipCharm offers a range of fonts to choose from, allowing you to match the text style to your project's theme.

- Color and Highlighting: Change the text color or add highlights to emphasize key points. Use the color palette or enter specific color codes for precise customization.

- Alignment and Spacing: Modify text alignment (left, center, right) and adjust line spacing or paragraph spacing to ensure readability and visual appeal.

2. Formatting Options

- Bold, Italic, Underline: Apply these basic formatting options to emphasize important text.

- Bullets and Numbering: Create lists to organize information clearly and effectively.

- Text Boxes and Shapes: Add text boxes or shapes around text to enhance visual presentation or to create callouts.

Image Editing and Customization

Images can significantly impact the effectiveness of a clip. ClipCharm provides tools for detailed image editing and customization:

1. Basic Image Adjustments

 - Crop and Resize: Adjust the size and shape of your image by cropping out unnecessary parts or resizing it to fit within your clip.

 - Rotate and Flip: Rotate images to the desired angle or flip them horizontally or vertically for better alignment.

2. Advanced Image Editing

 - Filters and Effects: Apply filters to change the image's appearance, such as adjusting brightness, contrast, or applying artistic effects.

 - Border and Shadows: Add borders or shadows to make your image stand out and add depth.

 - Overlay and Transparency: Use overlays to add additional elements to your image and adjust transparency levels to create a layered effect.

3. Image Enhancement

 - Adjust Colors: Modify color settings to correct image tones or match them with your clip's theme.

 - Add Text and Graphics: Overlay text or graphic elements onto images to provide additional context or branding.

Audio Editing and Customization

For clips that include audio, ClipCharm offers several tools to edit and customize sound elements:

1. Basic Audio Editing

 - Trim and Cut: Remove unnecessary parts of the audio track by trimming or cutting segments.

 - Adjust Volume: Increase or decrease the audio volume to ensure clarity and balance.

2. Advanced Audio Features

 - Fade In and Out: Apply fade-in and fade-out effects to make transitions smoother.

 - Audio Effects: Add effects such as echo or reverb to enhance the audio experience.

 - Noise Reduction: Use noise reduction tools to eliminate background noise and improve audio quality.

Video Editing and Customization

If your clip includes video content, ClipCharm's video editing tools will help you enhance and refine your footage:

1. Basic Video Editing

 - Trim and Split: Cut out unwanted sections of the video or split it into multiple clips.

 - Merge Clips: Combine multiple video clips into a single cohesive video.

2. Advanced Video Customization

 - Transitions and Effects: Add transitions between video segments and apply visual effects to enhance the overall presentation.

 - Adjust Speed: Modify the playback speed of your video, including slow motion or fast forward effects.

 - Add Text and Annotations: Overlay text or annotations onto your video to provide additional information or commentary.

Customizing Clip Templates

ClipCharm also allows you to customize pre-made templates to fit your specific needs:

1. Selecting a Template

- Browse the available templates in ClipCharm's template library and choose one that suits your project.

2. Modifying Template Elements

- Text Fields: Replace placeholder text with your content, and adjust text formatting as needed.

- Images and Graphics: Replace template images with your own and adjust their placement and size.

- Colors and Styles: Customize the color scheme and styles to match your branding or personal preferences.

Saving and Applying Changes

Once you've made your edits and customizations, it's important to save your work properly:

1. Saving Edits

- Click the "Save" button to preserve your changes. ClipCharm may also offer options to save your clip as a new version, allowing you to retain the original if needed.

2. Previewing Changes

- Before finalizing, use the preview function to review your edits and ensure everything appears as intended.

3. Exporting Clips

- Export your customized clip in the desired format, suitable for sharing or integration into other projects.

Best Practices for Effective Editing

1. Maintain Consistency

- Ensure that all clips follow a consistent style and formatting to create a cohesive look across your project.

2. Keep It Simple

- Avoid overcomplicating clips with excessive effects or elements. Aim for clarity and simplicity to communicate your message effectively.

3. Test and Review

- Always test your edited clips and review them to ensure they meet your quality standards before finalizing and sharing.

3.2 Managing Your Clip Library

Managing your Clip Library effectively is crucial for maintaining productivity and ensuring that your clips are easily accessible when you need them. This section will delve into the best practices for organizing your clips, helping you to create a streamlined and efficient system.

3.2.1 Organizing Clips

Organizing your clips within ClipCharm is essential for efficient workflow and ease of access. A well-organized Clip Library can save you significant time and effort, particularly when you are dealing with a large number of clips. Here are several strategies and tips for organizing your clips effectively:

1. Creating a Clear Folder Structure

The first step in organizing your clips is to establish a clear folder structure. This structure should be intuitive and reflect the way you think about your content. Here are some tips for creating a folder structure:

- By Project: Create folders for each project you are working on. Within each project folder, you can create subfolders for different types of content or different stages of the project.

- By Date: If you work on recurring projects or content that needs to be updated regularly, organizing by date can be very effective. Create folders for each year, month, or week, and store clips accordingly.

- By Content Type: Organize your clips by the type of content they represent, such as videos, images, documents, or presentations. This can make it easier to find specific types of content quickly.

2. Naming Conventions

Consistent naming conventions are crucial for keeping your Clip Library organized. Here are some guidelines for naming your clips:

- Descriptive Names: Use descriptive names that clearly indicate the content of the clip. Avoid generic names like "Clip1" or "Untitled".

- Include Dates: Including the date in the clip name can help you keep track of when the clip was created or last updated. Use a consistent date format, such as YYYY-MM-DD.

- Version Numbers: If you frequently update your clips, consider adding version numbers to the names. This will help you keep track of different iterations of the same content.

3. Tagging and Metadata

Tagging and metadata are powerful tools for organizing and searching your clips. ClipCharm allows you to add tags and metadata to your clips, making it easier to categorize and find them later.

- Use Relevant Tags: Tag your clips with relevant keywords that describe the content, purpose, or context of the clip. Think about how you might search for the clip in the future.

- Standardize Tags: Develop a standard set of tags and use them consistently. This will make it easier to find related clips and ensure that your tags are meaningful.

- Add Descriptions: Use the description field to add more context to your clips. This can be particularly useful for longer clips or clips that may not be fully described by their name and tags alone.

4. Archiving Old Clips

As you accumulate more clips, it's important to periodically review and archive old or unused clips. Archiving helps keep your Clip Library manageable and reduces clutter.

- Set Archiving Criteria: Determine criteria for when a clip should be archived, such as age, last accessed date, or project completion.

- Create an Archive Folder: Move archived clips to a dedicated archive folder. This keeps them out of your main working folders but still accessible if needed.

- Regularly Review Archives: Periodically review your archive folder to see if any clips can be permanently deleted or if any need to be restored to active use.

5. Utilizing ClipCharm Features

ClipCharm offers several features that can aid in organizing your clips effectively. Make use of these features to streamline your organization process:

- Clip Collections: Create collections for related clips. Collections can act as a virtual grouping, allowing you to gather clips from different folders without moving them.

- Favorites: Mark frequently used clips as favorites for quick access. This is especially useful for clips you use in multiple projects or on a regular basis.

- Filters and Views: Use filters and different view options within ClipCharm to sort and display your clips in ways that make sense for your workflow.

6. Maintaining Consistency

Consistency is key to keeping your Clip Library organized over the long term. Develop habits and routines to ensure that your clips remain well-organized.

- Regular Maintenance: Set aside regular times to review and organize your Clip Library. This could be weekly, monthly, or at the end of each project.

- Stay Disciplined: Be disciplined about following your naming conventions, tagging rules, and folder structure. Consistency will make organization easier in the long run.

- Educate Your Team: If you are working in a collaborative environment, ensure that all team members understand and follow the organizational rules you've set up.

7. Backup and Security

Ensuring that your clips are backed up and secure is also a crucial part of managing your Clip Library. Clips can be valuable assets, and losing them can be detrimental to your projects.

- Regular Backups: Set up regular backups of your Clip Library to prevent data loss. Use cloud storage solutions for automated and reliable backups.

- Access Controls: Implement access controls to ensure that only authorized personnel can modify or delete clips. This helps maintain the integrity of your Clip Library.

8. Using Search Functions

ClipCharm's search functionality is a powerful tool for finding and organizing your clips. Here are some tips for making the most of it:

- Keyword Searches: Use specific keywords that you've included in your clip names, tags, and descriptions to quickly locate clips.

- Advanced Search Filters: Take advantage of advanced search filters to narrow down your search results by date, tag, content type, or other criteria.

- Saved Searches: Save frequent searches for quick access. This can be particularly useful if you regularly search for the same types of clips.

9. Leveraging Templates

Using templates can save you time and ensure consistency across your clips. ClipCharm allows you to create and use templates for common clip types.

- Create Templates: Develop templates for frequently used clip formats. This could include specific layouts, tags, and naming conventions.

- Standardize Templates: Use standardized templates to ensure that all clips of a certain type have a consistent look and feel.

10. Collaborative Organization

If you are working in a team, collaboration is key to maintaining an organized Clip Library. Here are some tips for collaborative organization:

- Shared Folders: Use shared folders for team projects. Ensure that all team members understand the folder structure and naming conventions.

- Role-Based Access: Assign roles and permissions to team members based on their responsibilities. This helps prevent accidental modifications or deletions.

- Communication: Regularly communicate with your team about the organization of the Clip Library. Hold meetings or training sessions to ensure everyone is on the same page.

By following these strategies and tips, you can create an organized and efficient Clip Library in ClipCharm. This will not only save you time but also enhance your productivity and collaboration with team members.

3.2.2 Searching and Filtering Clips

Managing a large collection of clips can become overwhelming if you don't have efficient ways to search and filter through them. ClipCharm in Microsoft 365 provides robust tools to help you quickly locate the clips you need, ensuring that your workflow remains smooth and productive. In this section, we will explore various methods and strategies for searching and filtering clips within ClipCharm.

Understanding the Search Functionality

ClipCharm's search functionality is designed to be intuitive and powerful, allowing you to find clips based on a variety of criteria. Here are the key components of the search functionality:

- Search Bar: The search bar is typically located at the top of the ClipCharm interface. This is where you enter keywords or phrases to find specific clips.

- Search Filters: To refine your search results, ClipCharm offers several filters that you can apply. These filters help narrow down the search results based on specific attributes of the clips.

Performing a Basic Search

To perform a basic search in ClipCharm, follow these steps:

1. Access the Search Bar: Locate the search bar at the top of the ClipCharm interface.

2. Enter Keywords: Type in the keywords or phrases related to the clip you are looking for. For example, if you are searching for clips related to a specific project, you might enter the project name or relevant terms.

3. View Results: Press Enter or click the search icon to view the search results. ClipCharm will display a list of clips that match your search criteria.

Using Advanced Search Filters

For more precise searching, ClipCharm provides advanced search filters. These filters allow you to narrow down your search results based on specific attributes of the clips. Here are some common filters you can use:

- Date Range: Filter clips based on the date they were created or last modified.

- Tags: Use tags to find clips that have been categorized under specific labels.

- Author: Search for clips created by a particular team member.

- File Type: Filter clips by their file type, such as text, image, or video.

To use advanced search filters, follow these steps:

1. Access Advanced Search: Click on the filter icon next to the search bar to open the advanced search options.

2. Select Filters: Choose the filters you want to apply. For example, you can select a date range to find clips created within the last month.

3. Apply Filters: Click the "Apply" button to refine your search results. The clips that match your criteria will be displayed.

Combining Keywords and Filters

One of the most powerful features of ClipCharm's search functionality is the ability to combine keywords and filters. This allows you to perform highly targeted searches. For example, you can enter a keyword related to a project and apply a filter to only show clips created by a specific team member within the last week.

Saving Search Queries

If you frequently search for the same types of clips, ClipCharm allows you to save your search queries. This can save you time and effort by allowing you to quickly access saved searches. To save a search query, follow these steps:

1. Perform a Search: Enter your search criteria and apply any filters as needed.

2. Save the Search: Click on the "Save Search" button, usually located near the search bar.

3. Name the Search: Give your saved search a meaningful name, such as "Weekly Project Updates."

4. Access Saved Searches: To use a saved search, click on the "Saved Searches" menu and select the desired query.

Using Tags for Effective Filtering

Tags are a powerful way to categorize and filter clips in ClipCharm. By assigning tags to your clips, you can create a more organized and searchable library. Here are some tips for using tags effectively:

- Consistent Tagging: Establish a consistent tagging system for your team. This ensures that everyone uses the same tags, making it easier to find clips.

- Multiple Tags: Assign multiple tags to each clip to improve searchability. For example, a clip related to a marketing campaign can have tags like "Marketing," "Campaign," and "Q3 2024."

- Review and Update Tags: Periodically review and update your tags to ensure they remain relevant. Remove obsolete tags and add new ones as needed.

Filtering by Tag

To filter clips by tag, follow these steps:

1. Open the Filter Menu: Click on the filter icon next to the search bar.

2. Select Tags: Choose the tags you want to filter by from the list of available tags.

3. Apply Filter: Click the "Apply" button to view clips that match the selected tags.

Using the ClipCharm Library for Team Collaboration

ClipCharm's library is not only a repository for your clips but also a collaborative tool for your team. By efficiently managing and searching for clips, you can enhance team collaboration and productivity. Here are some collaborative features to consider:

- Shared Tags: Create shared tags for team projects. This ensures that all team members can quickly find and use relevant clips.

- Shared Searches: Save and share search queries with your team. This allows everyone to benefit from frequently used search criteria.

- Real-Time Collaboration: Use ClipCharm's real-time collaboration features to work together on clip projects. Team members can search for clips, make edits, and provide feedback within the platform.

Tips for Effective Clip Management

Effective clip management involves more than just searching and filtering. Here are some additional tips to help you manage your clip library:

- Regularly Organize Clips: Set aside time each week to organize your clips. This can involve adding tags, archiving old clips, and removing duplicates.

- Use Descriptive Names: Give your clips descriptive names that make them easy to identify. Avoid generic names like "Clip 1" or "Project Video."

- Backup Your Library: Regularly backup your ClipCharm library to prevent data loss. This can be done through Microsoft 365's backup features or external storage solutions.

- Training and Documentation: Provide training for your team on using ClipCharm's search and filtering features. Create documentation or guides to help new team members get up to speed.

Common Challenges and Solutions

Managing a clip library can come with challenges. Here are some common issues and solutions:

- Large Volume of Clips: As your library grows, finding specific clips can become difficult. Use advanced search filters and regularly review your tags to keep your library manageable.

- Inconsistent Tagging: Inconsistent tagging can lead to confusion and difficulty finding clips. Establish a tagging policy and train your team on its importance.

- Outdated Clips: Over time, some clips may become outdated. Regularly review and archive or delete old clips to keep your library current.

Conclusion

Efficiently searching and filtering clips in ClipCharm is essential for maintaining a well-organized and productive clip library. By understanding and utilizing the search functionality, advanced filters, and tagging system, you can quickly locate the clips you need and enhance team collaboration. Regular maintenance and consistent practices will ensure that your clip library remains a valuable resource for your projects and workflows.

3.3 Collaborating on Clip Projects

Effective collaboration is key to maximizing productivity and ensuring that everyone on the team is aligned and informed. ClipCharm offers robust features to facilitate seamless collaboration on clip projects within Microsoft 365, making it easier for teams to work together, share insights, and achieve their goals. This section will explore how to share clips with team members, ensuring that everyone can contribute and benefit from the collective effort.

3.3.1 Sharing Clips with Team Members

Sharing clips with team members in ClipCharm is straightforward and intuitive, thanks to its integration with Microsoft 365's suite of collaborative tools. Whether you're working on a project with colleagues in the same office or collaborating with a global team, ClipCharm's sharing features ensure that your clips are accessible to those who need them.

Step-by-Step Guide to Sharing Clips

1. Select the Clip to Share:

 Begin by selecting the clip you want to share from your Clip Library. You can do this by navigating to the library, finding the clip, and clicking on it to open the detailed view.

2. Access the Sharing Options:

 In the detailed view of the clip, locate the sharing icon or button, typically represented by an icon resembling a paper airplane or share symbol. Clicking on this will open the sharing options menu.

3. Choose the Recipients:

 In the sharing menu, you will see a field where you can enter the email addresses of the team members you want to share the clip with. If your organization uses Microsoft 365, you can often select names from your contact list or directory, making it easier to find the right people.

4. Set Permissions:

ClipCharm allows you to set different levels of access permissions for each recipient. You can choose to give them view-only access, allowing them to watch the clip without making any changes, or you can grant edit permissions, enabling them to make modifications and contribute to the clip.

5. Add a Message (Optional):

When sharing a clip, you may also add a personal message or instructions for your team members. This can help provide context or highlight specific areas of the clip that need attention.

6. Send the Invitation:

Once you've set the permissions and added any necessary messages, click the "Send" or "Share" button to send the invitation. Your team members will receive an email notification with a link to access the clip.

Best Practices for Sharing Clips

To ensure that your team collaboration is as effective as possible, consider these best practices when sharing clips in ClipCharm:

- Provide Clear Instructions: When sharing clips, especially if they require feedback or edits, include clear instructions on what is expected from the recipients. This helps avoid confusion and ensures that everyone knows their role and responsibilities.

- Use Descriptive Titles and Tags: Make your clips easy to find and understand by using descriptive titles and relevant tags. This is particularly useful for large teams or projects with numerous clips, as it helps team members quickly locate the clips they need.

- Set Appropriate Permissions: Be mindful of the permissions you grant to each team member. View-only access is suitable for informational clips, while edit permissions should be given to those who need to collaborate actively on the content.

- Encourage Feedback and Discussion: Use the comment features available in ClipCharm to encourage team members to provide feedback and engage in discussions about the clips. This fosters a collaborative environment and can lead to improved content quality.

Utilizing Microsoft 365 Integration for Sharing

ClipCharm's integration with Microsoft 365 enhances the sharing experience by leveraging the collaborative tools available within the platform. Here's how you can make the most of this integration:

- Microsoft Teams: Share clips directly in Microsoft Teams channels or chats to keep all project-related communication in one place. Team members can watch the clips, leave comments, and discuss them in real-time.

- SharePoint: Store and share clips within SharePoint libraries to take advantage of its document management capabilities. SharePoint's version control features can also help track changes and maintain a history of the clip's evolution.

- Outlook: Use Outlook to send clips as part of your email communication. This is particularly useful for reaching team members who may not be actively using ClipCharm but need to view the clips.

- OneDrive: Save and share clips via OneDrive to ensure they are accessible from anywhere, on any device. OneDrive's synchronization features make it easy to keep your clips up-to-date and available offline.

Real-World Scenarios and Use Cases

Scenario 1: Marketing Team Collaboration

A marketing team is working on a new campaign and needs to create several promotional videos. Using ClipCharm, the team leader creates the initial drafts of the clips and shares them with the team for feedback. Team members review the clips, leave comments, and suggest edits. The team leader incorporates the feedback and shares the revised clips. This iterative process continues until the final versions are approved.

Scenario 2: Training and Onboarding

A company is onboarding new employees and has created a series of training clips using ClipCharm. The HR department shares these clips with the new hires, granting view-only access. The new employees can watch the clips at their own pace and refer back to them as needed. HR can also track which clips have been viewed and follow up with any additional training if necessary.

Scenario 3: Project Management

A project manager is overseeing a complex project that involves multiple departments. To ensure everyone is aligned, the manager creates clips outlining key project milestones and requirements. These clips are shared with all team members via Microsoft Teams. The project manager sets up regular review meetings where the team watches the clips together and discusses any updates or changes.

Troubleshooting Common Issues

While sharing clips in ClipCharm is generally straightforward, you may encounter some common issues:

- Email Notifications Not Received: If team members do not receive email notifications, ask them to check their spam or junk folders. Ensure that ClipCharm's email domain is whitelisted in your organization's email system.

- Access Permissions: If team members cannot access the clips, verify that the correct permissions have been set. Double-check the email addresses to ensure there are no typos.

- Technical Glitches: In case of technical issues, such as clips not loading properly, try clearing your browser cache or using a different browser. Contact ClipCharm support if the problem persists.

Conclusion

Sharing clips with team members in ClipCharm is an essential aspect of effective collaboration. By following the steps outlined in this section and adhering to best practices, you can ensure that your team can easily access, review, and contribute to clip projects. Leveraging Microsoft 365's integration further enhances the sharing experience, making it a seamless part of your organization's workflow. Whether you are working on marketing campaigns, training programs, or complex projects, ClipCharm's sharing features will help you collaborate more efficiently and achieve better results.

3.3.2 Collaborative Editing

Collaborative editing is a powerful feature of ClipCharm that allows multiple users to work together on clip projects in real-time. This section delves into the nuances of collaborative editing within ClipCharm, providing a comprehensive guide to effectively utilize this feature for enhanced teamwork and productivity.

Overview of Collaborative Editing

Collaborative editing enables users to simultaneously edit and review clips, ensuring that team projects are completed efficiently and accurately. This feature is particularly valuable for teams working on content creation, document preparation, and other collaborative tasks within Microsoft 365. By leveraging ClipCharm's collaborative editing capabilities, users can streamline workflows, improve communication, and achieve better results.

Setting Up Collaborative Editing

1. Inviting Team Members:

- To begin collaborative editing, the primary user must invite team members to join the clip project. This process involves selecting the clip or project to be edited and choosing the "Share" or "Invite" option from the ClipCharm interface.

- Users can invite team members via email or by sharing a unique invitation link. It's important to ensure that all invited members have the appropriate permissions to edit the clip.

2. Defining Permissions:

- Permissions play a crucial role in collaborative editing. ClipCharm provides various permission levels, such as "Can Edit," "Can Comment," and "Can View."

- The primary user should carefully assign these permissions based on the roles and responsibilities of each team member. For example, contributors who need to make changes should be granted "Can Edit" access, while others who only need to provide feedback might receive "Can Comment" access.

3. Setting Up Real-Time Collaboration:

- Once team members are invited and permissions are set, ClipCharm facilitates real-time collaboration. This means that all changes made by any team member are instantly visible to others working on the same clip or project.

- Users can track changes using ClipCharm's version history feature, which records edits and allows for the restoration of previous versions if needed.

Best Practices for Effective Collaborative Editing

1. Establish Clear Guidelines:

- Before starting collaborative editing, it's essential to establish clear guidelines and expectations for the team. This includes defining roles, responsibilities, and deadlines.

- Clear communication about the scope of the project and the specific contributions expected from each team member helps prevent confusion and overlapping efforts.

2. Utilize Commenting and Annotations:

- ClipCharm includes features for commenting and annotating clips, which are crucial for providing feedback and making suggestions during the collaborative editing process.

- Team members should use these features to leave constructive comments, highlight areas for improvement, and discuss potential changes. This approach ensures that feedback is organized and easily accessible.

3. Manage Conflicts and Overlaps:

- Collaborative editing may sometimes lead to conflicts or overlaps in contributions. For instance, if two team members make changes to the same section of a clip simultaneously, it can result in conflicts.

- ClipCharm helps manage these situations by providing tools for conflict resolution. Users can review conflicting changes and decide which version to keep or merge.

4. Regularly Save and Review Changes:

- Regularly saving changes is crucial in collaborative editing to avoid data loss and ensure that all contributions are recorded.

- Periodic reviews of the clip's progress help maintain alignment with project goals and identify any issues early on.

5. Use Notifications and Alerts:

- ClipCharm offers notification and alert features to keep team members informed about updates, comments, and changes.

- Enabling these notifications ensures that everyone stays up-to-date with the latest developments and can respond promptly to any new input.

Advanced Features in Collaborative Editing

1. Version Control:

- ClipCharm's version control feature allows users to track changes over time and revert to previous versions if necessary. This is particularly useful for managing complex projects with multiple contributors.

- Users can view the version history to see who made specific changes and when, providing transparency and accountability.

2. Integration with Microsoft 365 Tools:

- ClipCharm integrates seamlessly with other Microsoft 365 tools, such as Word, Excel, and Teams. This integration enhances the collaborative editing experience by allowing users to work across different platforms.

- For example, team members can link ClipCharm clips to Microsoft Teams channels for easier access and discussion.

3. Synchronization Across Devices:

- ClipCharm's cloud-based architecture ensures that collaborative edits are synchronized across all devices. Whether team members are working on desktops, laptops, or mobile devices, they can access and contribute to the project in real-time.

Addressing Challenges in Collaborative Editing

1. Handling Discrepancies in Contributions:

- When multiple users are involved, discrepancies in contributions can arise. For instance, different team members might have varying styles or preferences.

- Establishing a clear style guide and providing training on ClipCharm's features can help minimize discrepancies and ensure consistency in the final output.

2. Managing Large Teams:

- Collaborating with a large team can be challenging, especially when coordinating contributions and maintaining clear communication.

- Using ClipCharm's project management tools, such as task assignments and deadlines, helps manage large teams effectively and keep everyone on track.

3. Ensuring Data Security and Privacy:

- Collaborative editing involves sharing sensitive information, so ensuring data security and privacy is paramount.

- ClipCharm provides robust security features, such as encrypted data transmission and secure access controls, to protect your information.

Conclusion

Collaborative editing in ClipCharm offers a powerful way to enhance teamwork and streamline content creation within Microsoft 365. By setting up collaborative editing effectively, adhering to best practices, and leveraging advanced features, teams can work together seamlessly and achieve their project goals. Addressing challenges and utilizing the tools available will ensure a smooth and productive collaborative editing experience.

CHAPTER IV
Advanced ClipCharm Features

4.1 Integrating ClipCharm with Other Microsoft 365 Tools

4.1.1 Integration with Word and Excel

Integrating ClipCharm with Microsoft Word and Excel can significantly enhance your productivity and streamline your workflow. This section provides a comprehensive guide on how to effectively integrate ClipCharm with these essential Microsoft 365 tools.

Overview of Integration Benefits

The integration of ClipCharm with Word and Excel allows you to seamlessly manage, share, and utilize clips (text, images, data) across different documents and spreadsheets. This integration facilitates:

- Enhanced Efficiency: Quickly insert and manipulate clips without switching between applications.

- Consistent Formatting: Maintain uniformity in document and spreadsheet formatting.

- Improved Collaboration: Share clips easily with colleagues working on the same documents or spreadsheets.

Integrating ClipCharm with Microsoft Word

1. Linking Clips to Word Documents

1. Installing the ClipCharm Add-in for Word:

- To start, ensure you have the ClipCharm add-in installed in Microsoft Word. You can find this by navigating to the "Insert" tab, selecting "Get Add-ins," and searching for ClipCharm.

- Once installed, the ClipCharm add-in will appear on your Word toolbar.

2. Accessing Clips in Word:

  - Open your Word document and click on the ClipCharm icon in the toolbar.

  - A sidebar will appear, displaying your ClipCharm library, including all saved clips. This sidebar allows you to search for specific clips, organize them into folders, and view clip details.

3. Inserting Clips into Your Document:

  - To insert a clip, simply drag and drop it from the ClipCharm sidebar into your document.

  - You can also right-click on a clip and choose "Insert" from the context menu. This action will place the clip directly at the cursor's position in the document.

4. Editing and Formatting Clips:

  - Once a clip is inserted, you can edit and format it just like any other content in Word.

  - For text clips, use Word's text formatting options to adjust font size, style, and color.

  - For image clips, you can resize, crop, or apply effects using Word's image tools.

 2. Utilizing ClipCharm Templates

1. Creating Templates:

  - You can create reusable templates in ClipCharm for frequently used document elements. For instance, if you often use certain headings, footers, or boilerplate text, save these as clips in ClipCharm.

  - To create a template, simply save your formatted content as a clip in ClipCharm.

2. Applying Templates in Word:

  - To use a template, open the ClipCharm sidebar and locate your saved templates.

  - Drag and drop the template clip into your Word document to quickly insert standardized content.

3. Updating Templates:

  - If you need to make changes to a template, edit the clip in ClipCharm and save the updated version.

  - Any document that uses this template will reflect the changes when the clip is updated.

3. Collaborating with Clips in Word

1. Sharing Clips with Team Members:

  - ClipCharm allows you to share specific clips or entire folders with colleagues.

  - In the ClipCharm sidebar, select the clip or folder you wish to share, click on the share icon, and choose the sharing options (e.g., email, link, or shared workspace).

2. Collaborative Editing:

  - When collaborating on a Word document, team members can access and insert shared clips into their own sections of the document.

  - This ensures that everyone is using the latest version of clips and maintains consistency across the document.

Integrating ClipCharm with Microsoft Excel

1. Linking Clips to Excel Spreadsheets

1. Installing the ClipCharm Add-in for Excel:

  - Similar to Word, install the ClipCharm add-in for Excel through the "Insert" tab by selecting "Get Add-ins" and searching for ClipCharm.

  - Once installed, the ClipCharm add-in will appear on your Excel ribbon.

2. Accessing Clips in Excel:

  - Open your Excel workbook and click on the ClipCharm icon in the ribbon.

  - A sidebar will display your ClipCharm library, allowing you to browse, search, and manage your clips.

3. Inserting Clips into Cells:

- To insert a clip, drag and drop it from the ClipCharm sidebar into the desired cell.

- For text clips, the content will populate the selected cell. For image clips, the image will be placed within the cell or range of cells.

4. Editing and Formatting Clips:

  - Edit text clips directly within the cell using Excel's text editing tools.

  - Image clips can be resized or formatted using Excel's image tools, ensuring they fit within the cell or range as needed.

2. Using ClipCharm for Data Management

1. Creating Data Templates:

  - Save commonly used data sets or formulas as clips in ClipCharm. This is particularly useful for recurring financial models, reports, or data structures.

  - To create a data template, enter your data or formula in Excel, then save it as a clip in ClipCharm.

2. Applying Data Templates in Excel:

  - To use a data template, access the ClipCharm sidebar, locate the desired clip, and drag it into the appropriate cells in your Excel workbook.

  - This feature allows for quick insertion of standardized data without manually re-entering information.

3. Updating Data Templates:

  - Update data templates by modifying the clip in ClipCharm. Changes will be reflected wherever the clip has been used, ensuring consistency across multiple spreadsheets.

3. Collaborating with Clips in Excel

1. Sharing Clips with Team Members:

  - Similar to Word, share specific data clips or entire folders with team members.

- Use the share icon in the ClipCharm sidebar to select sharing options such as email or shared workspaces.

2. Collaborative Data Editing:

  - Team members can insert and use shared data clips in their own workbooks or sheets.

  - This collaborative approach ensures that all team members have access to the latest data and templates.

Best Practices for Integration

1. Consistency in Clip Formatting:

  - Maintain consistent formatting for clips used in Word and Excel to ensure a professional and uniform appearance across documents and spreadsheets.

2. Regularly Update Clips:

  - Keep your clips updated with the latest information and formats. Regularly review and revise clips to ensure they meet current needs and standards.

3. Organize Clips Effectively:

  - Use folders and tags in ClipCharm to organize your clips efficiently. This organization helps you quickly locate and manage clips as your library grows.

4. Leverage Automation:

  - Utilize ClipCharm's automation features to streamline the process of inserting and updating clips in Word and Excel. Set up automation rules to enhance productivity and reduce manual tasks.

Troubleshooting Common Issues

1. ClipCharm Add-in Not Appearing:

  - If the ClipCharm add-in is not visible in Word or Excel, ensure it is properly installed and enabled. Go to "Add-ins" settings in Microsoft 365 to check its status.

2. Inserting Clips Results in Formatting Issues:

- If formatting issues occur, verify that the clip's formatting is compatible with the target document or spreadsheet. Adjust formatting settings in Word or Excel as needed.

3. Clip Sharing Problems:

- If you encounter issues with sharing clips, check your sharing permissions and network connectivity. Ensure that the recipient has access to the shared clips or folders.

Conclusion

Integrating ClipCharm with Microsoft Word and Excel can dramatically enhance your efficiency and collaboration capabilities. By following the guidelines outlined in this section, you can leverage ClipCharm's features to streamline document creation, data management, and team collaboration. Regular updates and effective organization of clips will ensure that you make the most out of this powerful integration, contributing to a more productive and cohesive work environment.

4.1.2 Using ClipCharm with Teams and SharePoint

Introduction

Microsoft Teams and SharePoint are two powerful tools within the Microsoft 365 suite that facilitate collaboration, communication, and document management. Integrating ClipCharm with these tools can significantly enhance your productivity by streamlining workflows and making it easier to manage and share content. This section will guide you through the process of integrating ClipCharm with Microsoft Teams and SharePoint, highlighting the benefits and providing step-by-step instructions for a seamless experience.

Benefits of Integration

Integrating ClipCharm with Teams and SharePoint offers several advantages:

1. Enhanced Collaboration: ClipCharm's functionality to create, manage, and share clips can be extended to Teams and SharePoint, making collaboration more efficient and effective.

2. Streamlined Workflows: Automation and integration with these tools reduce the need for manual updates and ensure that all team members have access to the latest content.

3. Centralized Access: By integrating ClipCharm, you can centralize your content management within Teams and SharePoint, providing a single source of truth for your team.

Using ClipCharm with Microsoft Teams

1. Integrating ClipCharm Tabs into Teams

One of the simplest ways to integrate ClipCharm with Teams is by adding it as a tab within a Team channel. This allows team members to access ClipCharm features directly from their Teams workspace.

Step-by-Step Guide:

1. Navigate to Your Team: Open Microsoft Teams and go to the team where you want to add ClipCharm.

2. Add a Tab: Click on the "+" icon at the top of the channel to add a new tab.

3. Select ClipCharm: In the list of available apps, select ClipCharm. If ClipCharm is not listed, you may need to configure it or use a custom web tab.

4. Configure the Tab: Follow the prompts to configure the ClipCharm tab. This may include logging in to your ClipCharm account and selecting the specific clips or libraries you want to display.

5. Save and Share: Once configured, save the tab. Team members can now view and interact with ClipCharm content directly within Teams.

2. Sharing Clips in Teams Conversations

ClipCharm clips can be shared directly within Teams conversations, making it easy to collaborate on content.

Step-by-Step Guide:

1. Create or Select a Clip: In ClipCharm, create a new clip or select an existing one that you want to share.

2. Copy Clip URL: Copy the URL of the clip from ClipCharm.

3. Paste in Teams: Go to your Teams conversation and paste the clip URL. Teams will automatically create a preview of the clip.

4. Add Context: Provide any additional context or instructions in the Teams message to ensure that team members understand the purpose of the clip.

3. Automating Tasks with ClipCharm in Teams

You can automate certain tasks involving ClipCharm content within Teams using Microsoft Power Automate.

Step-by-Step Guide:

1. Open Power Automate: Go to Microsoft Power Automate and sign in.

2. Create a New Flow: Click on "Create" to start a new flow.

3. Select a Trigger: Choose a trigger event that will initiate the flow, such as a new clip creation in ClipCharm.

4. Add Actions: Add actions to the flow, such as posting a message to a Teams channel with a link to the new clip.

5. Save and Test: Save your flow and test it to ensure that it works as expected.

Using ClipCharm with SharePoint

1. Integrating ClipCharm with SharePoint Document Libraries

Integrating ClipCharm with SharePoint allows you to manage and access ClipCharm clips directly from SharePoint document libraries.

Step-by-Step Guide:

1. Navigate to SharePoint: Open your SharePoint site and go to the document library where you want to integrate ClipCharm.

2. Add a New Web Part: Click on "Edit" to modify the page, and then select "Add a Web Part."

3. Select Embed Code: Choose the "Embed" web part and paste the embed code provided by ClipCharm.

4. Configure and Save: Configure the web part settings to display the desired ClipCharm clips and save the changes.

2. Creating a ClipCharm Library in SharePoint

You can create a dedicated library in SharePoint to store and manage ClipCharm clips, providing centralized access for your team.

Step-by-Step Guide:

1. Create a New Library: Go to your SharePoint site and create a new document library for ClipCharm clips.

2. Add ClipCharm Clips: Upload or link your ClipCharm clips to this library. You can also use SharePoint metadata to tag and categorize clips.

3. Configure Permissions: Set permissions for the library to control who can view and edit the ClipCharm clips.

3. Automating Workflows with ClipCharm and SharePoint

Automate workflows involving ClipCharm content and SharePoint using Power Automate to enhance productivity.

Step-by-Step Guide:

1. Open Power Automate: Access Microsoft Power Automate and sign in.

2. Create a New Flow: Start a new flow by clicking on "Create."

3. Select a Trigger: Choose a trigger event related to SharePoint, such as a new file added to a document library.

4. Add Actions: Add actions to the flow, such as creating a new ClipCharm clip or updating an existing one based on SharePoint changes.

5. Save and Test: Save the flow and test it to ensure it performs as expected.

Best Practices for Integration

1. Regularly Update Integrations: Ensure that your integrations are up-to-date with the latest features and improvements from ClipCharm, Teams, and SharePoint.

2. Train Your Team: Provide training to your team members on how to use ClipCharm effectively within Teams and SharePoint to maximize the benefits.

3. Monitor Performance: Regularly monitor the performance of your integrations to identify and address any issues or inefficiencies.

Conclusion

Integrating ClipCharm with Microsoft Teams and SharePoint can greatly enhance your productivity by streamlining workflows, improving collaboration, and centralizing content management. By following the steps outlined in this section, you can effectively leverage the power of ClipCharm within these Microsoft 365 tools and achieve a more efficient and collaborative work environment.

4.2 Automating Tasks with ClipCharm

4.2.1 Setting Up Automation Rules

Automation is a key feature of ClipCharm that can significantly enhance your productivity by minimizing manual effort and streamlining repetitive tasks. This section will guide you through the process of setting up automation rules in ClipCharm, ensuring you can harness its full potential to optimize your workflow.

Understanding Automation in ClipCharm

Automation in ClipCharm allows you to define rules and triggers that automatically perform actions based on specific conditions. This feature is designed to handle repetitive tasks, such as organizing clips, applying tags, or sending notifications, without requiring manual intervention. By setting up automation rules, you can ensure that your ClipCharm workspace remains organized and efficient, and you can focus more on your core tasks.

Step 1: Accessing the Automation Settings

To begin setting up automation rules, you first need to access the automation settings within ClipCharm:

1. Open ClipCharm: Launch the ClipCharm application from your Microsoft 365 suite.

2. Navigate to Settings: Go to the settings menu, usually accessible from the gear icon or the "Settings" tab in the navigation bar.

3. Select Automation: Within the settings menu, locate the "Automation" section. This is where you will configure and manage your automation rules.

Step 2: Creating a New Automation Rule

Once you're in the Automation section, follow these steps to create a new rule:

1. Click on 'Create New Rule': Look for a button or link labeled "Create New Rule" or something similar.

2. Define Rule Name and Description: Give your rule a descriptive name and provide a brief description of its purpose. This will help you identify and manage the rule later.

3. Set Up Triggers: A trigger is an event that initiates the automation rule. Click on "Add Trigger" to select the conditions that will activate the rule. Common triggers include:

  - New Clip Added: Trigger an action whenever a new clip is added to your library.

  - Tag Applied: Activate the rule when a specific tag is applied to a clip.

  - Date and Time: Set rules to run at specific times or intervals.

4. Specify Conditions: After selecting a trigger, define any additional conditions that must be met for the rule to execute. For example:

  - Clip Type: Apply the rule only to clips of a certain type or category.

  - Keywords: Specify keywords that must be present in the clip title or description.

Step 3: Defining Actions

Once you've set up your triggers and conditions, you need to define the actions that should be taken when the rule is triggered:

1. Click on 'Add Action': This will open a list of available actions that you can assign to your rule.

2. Choose Actions: Select the actions you want to automate. Common actions include:

  - Move Clip: Automatically move clips to a specific folder or category.

  - Apply Tag: Add or remove tags from clips based on predefined criteria.

  - Send Notification: Trigger notifications to inform team members of specific changes or updates.

  - Generate Report: Automatically create and send reports based on the clips and their attributes.

3. Configure Action Parameters: For each action, you may need to specify additional parameters. For instance, if you choose to move a clip, you'll need to select the destination folder.

Step 4: Testing the Automation Rule

Before fully implementing your automation rule, it's essential to test it to ensure it works as expected:

1. Save the Rule: Click "Save" to apply the rule settings.

2. Test Scenario: Perform an action that would trigger the rule. For example, add a new clip that meets the trigger criteria.

3. Review Results: Check whether the actions were executed as planned. Verify that clips were moved, tags were applied, or notifications were sent as expected.

Step 5: Managing and Updating Automation Rules

After setting up your automation rules, you'll need to manage and update them periodically:

1. Access Automation Management: Return to the Automation section in ClipCharm settings.

2. Review Existing Rules: View and edit your existing rules to ensure they continue to meet your needs.

3. Deactivate or Delete Rules: If a rule is no longer necessary, you can deactivate or delete it to avoid unnecessary processing.

Best Practices for Automation

To maximize the effectiveness of your automation rules, consider the following best practices:

1. Keep Rules Simple: Avoid creating overly complex rules that may conflict or lead to unintended consequences. Start with simple rules and gradually add complexity as needed.

2. Regularly Review Rules: Periodically review and adjust your rules to align with changing workflows or business requirements.

3. Document Rules: Maintain documentation of your automation rules, including their purpose, triggers, conditions, and actions. This will help you troubleshoot and modify rules as needed.

4. Monitor Performance: Pay attention to how well your automation rules are performing. If you notice any issues or inefficiencies, make adjustments to improve their effectiveness.

Examples of Automation Rules

To give you a better understanding of how automation can be applied in different scenarios, here are a few examples:

1. Organizing Clips by Category: Set up a rule to automatically move clips to specific folders based on their category or tags. For instance, you might have a rule that moves all "Marketing" clips to a "Marketing Campaigns" folder.

2. Tagging Clips by Date: Create a rule to apply tags to clips based on the date they were added. For example, clips added in January could be tagged with "January 2024."

3. Sending Notifications for New Clips: Implement a rule that sends a notification to your team whenever a new clip is added to a shared folder. This can help keep everyone informed about recent updates.

Conclusion

Setting up automation rules in ClipCharm can greatly enhance your efficiency and streamline your workflow. By understanding the triggers, conditions, and actions available, you can create rules that fit your specific needs and preferences. Regularly review and update your rules to ensure they continue to provide value, and remember to test thoroughly before implementing changes. With effective automation, you can focus on more strategic tasks while ClipCharm handles the routine aspects of managing your clips.

4.2.2 Examples of Automated Workflows

Automating tasks within ClipCharm can significantly enhance productivity by reducing manual effort and ensuring consistency in your processes. This section will explore practical examples of automated workflows that you can implement using ClipCharm in Microsoft 365. These workflows will help you streamline repetitive tasks, improve collaboration, and ensure that your processes are as efficient as possible.

1. Automated Content Creation and Distribution

Scenario: Your team frequently needs to create and distribute reports based on predefined templates.

Solution: You can automate the content creation and distribution process to save time and ensure consistency.

Steps:

1. Create a Report Template: Develop a standardized report template in ClipCharm. Ensure that it includes all necessary placeholders for dynamic content, such as charts, tables, and text sections.

2. Set Up Data Sources: Integrate ClipCharm with your data sources, such as Excel spreadsheets or databases, where the report data is stored. This integration ensures that the most up-to-date information is pulled into your reports.

3. Define Automation Rules:

   - Trigger: Schedule the automation to run at regular intervals (e.g., daily, weekly, monthly) or based on specific events (e.g., end of a project phase).

   - Action: Automate the generation of reports using the predefined template and data sources. Configure ClipCharm to populate the template with the latest data and generate a report.

4. Distribute the Report: Set up automation to email the generated report to the relevant stakeholders or upload it to a shared location (e.g., SharePoint, Teams).

Example Workflow:

- Daily sales reports are automatically generated from an Excel file containing sales data.

- The reports are formatted using a pre-designed template and sent via email to the sales team every morning.

2. Automated Task Assignments and Reminders

Scenario: Your team needs to assign tasks and set reminders for follow-up actions regularly.

Solution: Automate task assignments and reminders to ensure that tasks are distributed and followed up efficiently.

Steps:

1. Create Task Templates: Develop task templates in ClipCharm for common tasks that require regular assignment. Include standard instructions and deadlines in these templates.

2. Define Automation Rules:

   - Trigger: Set triggers based on specific events or dates (e.g., start of a new project, completion of a milestone).

   - Action: Automatically assign tasks to team members based on predefined criteria (e.g., roles, availability). Include deadlines and relevant details in the task assignments.

3. Set Up Reminders: Configure reminders to be sent to team members at predefined intervals (e.g., 1 day before the task deadline) to ensure that tasks are completed on time.

4. Track Task Progress: Use ClipCharm's tracking features to monitor the status of assigned tasks and automate follow-up actions if tasks are not completed on time.

Example Workflow:

- Weekly project tasks are automatically assigned to team members based on their roles and availability.

- Reminders are sent to each team member 24 hours before their task deadlines.

3. Automated Document Review and Approval

Scenario: Your organization needs to review and approve documents frequently, and you want to automate this process to improve efficiency.

Solution: Implement an automated workflow for document review and approval to streamline the process and reduce manual intervention.

Steps:

1. Create Review and Approval Templates: Develop templates for document review and approval workflows in ClipCharm. Define the steps involved, such as initial review, feedback, and final approval.

2. Define Automation Rules:

   - Trigger: Set triggers based on document creation or updates. For example, when a new document is uploaded to a shared folder.

   - Action: Automatically initiate the review process by sending the document to the designated reviewers and tracking their feedback.

3. Track Feedback and Approvals: Configure ClipCharm to collect feedback from reviewers and track the approval status. Automate reminders for reviewers who have not provided feedback within the specified timeframe.

4. Finalize Approval: Once all required approvals are obtained, automate the process of finalizing the document and notifying the relevant stakeholders.

Example Workflow:

- New marketing materials are automatically routed to the marketing team for review.

- Feedback and approval are tracked, and reminders are sent to reviewers who have not responded within the given timeframe.

4. Automated Data Synchronization and Reporting

Scenario: Your organization needs to synchronize data between different systems and generate reports based on that data.

Solution: Automate the data synchronization and reporting process to ensure that data is consistent and reports are generated efficiently.

Steps:

1. Set Up Data Integration: Integrate ClipCharm with your various data sources, such as CRM systems, databases, and spreadsheets. Ensure that data is synchronized across these systems.

2. Define Automation Rules:

 - Trigger: Schedule the synchronization to occur at regular intervals or based on specific events (e.g., new data entry).

 - Action: Automate the synchronization process to update data in real-time across all systems.

3. Generate Reports: Use ClipCharm to create reports based on the synchronized data. Set up automation to generate and distribute these reports to the relevant stakeholders.

4. Monitor Data Consistency: Implement checks to ensure that data is consistently synchronized and reports are accurate. Automate alerts for any discrepancies or errors.

Example Workflow:

- Customer data is synchronized between a CRM system and an internal database every night.

- Sales performance reports are generated based on the synchronized data and sent to the sales team each morning.

5. Automated Onboarding and Training

Scenario: Your organization frequently onboard new employees and provides them with training materials.

Solution: Automate the onboarding and training process to ensure that new hires receive the necessary information and resources efficiently.

Steps:

1. Create Onboarding Templates: Develop onboarding and training templates in ClipCharm that include essential information, training modules, and tasks for new employees.

2. Define Automation Rules:

 - Trigger: Set triggers based on new employee start dates or onboarding milestones.

- Action: Automatically send onboarding materials and training resources to new hires. Include instructions for completing training modules and tasks.

3. Track Progress: Use ClipCharm's tracking features to monitor the progress of new hires through the onboarding and training process. Automate reminders for any pending tasks or training modules.

4. Provide Support: Set up automation to provide additional support or resources to new hires based on their progress and feedback.

Example Workflow:

- New employees receive an automated onboarding package containing company information, training materials, and initial tasks on their first day.

- Progress is tracked, and reminders are sent for any incomplete training modules or tasks.

4.3 Customizing ClipCharm Settings

4.3.1 Personalizing Your Workspace

Personalizing your workspace in ClipCharm is essential for maximizing your efficiency and ensuring a comfortable and productive environment. Customizing the workspace allows you to tailor the tool to your specific needs and preferences, enhancing your overall experience with ClipCharm. This section will guide you through the various ways you can personalize your workspace in ClipCharm to suit your workflow and preferences.

1. Understanding the Workspace Layout

The ClipCharm workspace is designed to be flexible and adaptable to different user needs. The primary components of the workspace include:

- Dashboard: The main screen where you access recent clips, pinned items, and quick actions.

- Clip Library: A section for managing and organizing your clips.

- Toolbars: Located at the top or sides of the screen, these provide quick access to various functions and settings.

- Sidebar: This area can house shortcuts to frequently used features or modules.

- Search Bar: Allows for quick searching of clips and other resources.

Understanding these components is the first step in customizing your workspace effectively.

2. Customizing the Dashboard

The dashboard is the central hub of your ClipCharm experience. Here's how you can customize it:

2.1. Rearranging Widgets

- Accessing Widget Settings: Click on the "Customize" button or right-click on any widget to open its settings.

- Reordering Widgets: Drag and drop widgets to rearrange their position according to your preference.

- Adding/Removing Widgets: Use the "Add Widget" button to include additional widgets or click on the "Remove" icon to eliminate unnecessary ones.

2.2. Customizing Widget Content

- Widget Configuration: Each widget may offer settings to configure the content it displays. For example, the "Recent Clips" widget can be set to show clips from specific folders or tags.

- Setting Preferences: Adjust the widget preferences to display the most relevant information, such as the most frequently used clips or upcoming deadlines.

2.3. Using Themes and Layouts

- Selecting Themes: Choose from a range of pre-defined themes to match your personal style or organizational branding. Go to the "Theme Settings" to select or customize themes.

- Adjusting Layouts: Switch between different layout options (e.g., grid or list view) to find the one that best suits your workflow.

3. Organizing Your Clip Library

A well-organized Clip Library ensures that you can quickly find and manage your clips. Here's how to personalize it:

3.1. Creating Folders and Categories

- Adding Folders: Create folders to categorize your clips based on projects, teams, or topics. Right-click in the Clip Library section and select "New Folder."

- Subfolders and Hierarchies: Organize your folders into subfolders to create a hierarchical structure that mirrors your project organization.

3.2. Tagging and Labeling Clips

- Applying Tags: Use tags to label clips with relevant keywords. This makes searching and filtering easier. Tags can be added during the clip creation or editing process.

- Using Labels: Labels provide a way to group clips with similar attributes or purposes. Set up custom labels based on your needs.

3.3. Customizing Views and Sorting

- View Options: Customize how you view your clips by choosing between different view options such as list view, thumbnail view, or detailed view.

- Sorting Clips: Sort your clips based on criteria like date, name, or tag. This can be done from the "Sort" menu in the Clip Library section.

4. Configuring Toolbars and Shortcuts

Toolbars and shortcuts are crucial for efficient navigation and access to features. Here's how to configure them:

4.1. Customizing Toolbars

- Adding/Removing Tools: Go to "Toolbar Settings" to add or remove tools and functions from your toolbar. Choose tools that you use frequently for quicker access.

- Rearranging Toolbar Items: Drag and drop items on the toolbar to rearrange their order. This allows you to place the most-used tools in the most accessible positions.

4.2. Creating Keyboard Shortcuts

- Setting Shortcuts: Assign keyboard shortcuts to frequently used functions by accessing the "Keyboard Shortcuts" settings. This speeds up your workflow.

- Customizing Existing Shortcuts: Modify existing shortcuts if they conflict with other applications or if you prefer different key combinations.

5. Personalizing Sidebar and Search Features

The sidebar and search bar are essential for quick navigation and access to features. Here's how to personalize them:

5.1. Customizing the Sidebar

- Adding Shortcuts: Add shortcuts to your most-used features or folders by dragging them into the sidebar. This provides easy access to important areas of ClipCharm.

- Adjusting Sidebar Settings: Customize the sidebar's appearance and functionality by accessing "Sidebar Settings." Choose what information or shortcuts are displayed.

5.2. Enhancing Search Functionality

- Configuring Search Preferences: Adjust search settings to prioritize certain types of content or sources. This can be done in the "Search Settings" menu.

- Using Advanced Search Filters: Utilize advanced filters to refine search results based on criteria like tags, date ranges, or content types.

6. Personalizing Notifications and Alerts

Notifications and alerts keep you informed about important updates and activities. Here's how to customize them:

6.1. Managing Notification Settings

- Choosing Notification Types: Decide which types of notifications you want to receive (e.g., new clip updates, comments). Configure these settings in the "Notification Settings" menu.

- Setting Alert Preferences: Customize how and when you receive alerts. Choose between email notifications, in-app alerts, or desktop notifications.

6.2. Creating Custom Alerts

- Setting Up Custom Alerts: Create custom alerts for specific events or conditions, such as when a clip is edited or when a deadline approaches. Access this feature in the "Alert Settings" section.

7. Syncing and Integrating with Other Tools

Ensuring that ClipCharm integrates smoothly with other tools can enhance your productivity. Here's how to configure integrations:

7.1. Integrating with Microsoft 365 Applications

- Connecting with Outlook: Set up integration with Outlook to sync calendar events and email notifications. This can be done through the "Integration Settings" menu.

- Syncing with OneDrive: Link ClipCharm with OneDrive for seamless file access and synchronization.

7.2. Configuring Third-Party Integrations

- Connecting to External Tools: Configure integrations with third-party applications such as task management tools or project management software. This is done through the "External Integrations" settings.

8. Regular Maintenance and Updates

Maintaining your personalized settings ensures that ClipCharm continues to meet your needs effectively. Here's how to manage updates and maintenance:

8.1. Updating ClipCharm Settings

- Checking for Updates: Regularly check for updates to ClipCharm to ensure that you have the latest features and improvements. Go to "Update Settings" to see if updates are available.

- Applying New Features: Customize new features as they become available to keep your workspace up-to-date and aligned with your needs.

8.2. Performing Routine Maintenance

- Clearing Cache and Data: Periodically clear cache and temporary data to improve performance. This can be done through the "Maintenance" section in settings.

- Backing Up Settings: Regularly back up your personalized settings to avoid losing configurations. This can be done through the "Backup Settings" menu.

By personalizing your ClipCharm workspace, you can create a tailored environment that enhances your productivity and fits your unique workflow. This customization process not only improves your efficiency but also ensures a more enjoyable and effective use of ClipCharm within Microsoft 365.

4.3.2 Advanced Configuration Options

Customizing ClipCharm settings is crucial for tailoring the tool to meet the specific needs of users and optimizing their workflow within Microsoft 365. In this section, we will delve into the advanced configuration options available in ClipCharm, which offer deeper control over the functionality and appearance of the tool. By understanding and utilizing these advanced settings, users can enhance their productivity and ensure that ClipCharm aligns with their unique business processes and preferences.

User Profiles and Permissions

User Profiles

ClipCharm allows for extensive customization through user profiles. Each user profile can be configured to provide personalized settings, preferences, and permissions, which helps in managing different users' needs and roles within an organization.

- Creating User Profiles: Administrators can create and manage user profiles through the ClipCharm admin console. Each profile can be assigned specific settings that dictate the user's experience and access level within the application.

- Profile Customization: Users can customize their profiles by setting preferences for notifications, display options, and default actions. This personalization ensures that users interact with ClipCharm in a way that suits their work style.

Permissions Management

Permissions management is a critical aspect of configuring ClipCharm, particularly in collaborative environments where access control is important.

- Defining Access Levels: Administrators can define different access levels for various user roles. For example, some users may have read-only access, while others may have full editing and administrative rights.

- Customizing Permissions: Permissions can be customized at a granular level, allowing administrators to control who can view, edit, or delete specific clips, folders, or templates. This ensures that sensitive information is protected and only accessible to authorized individuals.

Advanced Automation Features

Setting Up Automation Rules

Automation in ClipCharm helps streamline repetitive tasks and enhance efficiency. Users can configure automation rules to automate various actions within the application.

- Creating Automation Rules: Users can set up rules based on specific triggers and conditions. For example, an automation rule can be created to automatically categorize clips based on predefined criteria, such as keywords or tags.

- Managing Automation Workflows: Automation workflows can be managed through a dedicated interface where users can view, edit, and delete existing rules. This interface also allows users to test and validate automation rules to ensure they function as expected.

Examples of Automated Workflows

Implementing automated workflows can significantly reduce manual intervention and improve consistency across processes. Here are a few examples of how automation can be used in ClipCharm:

- Clip Organization: Automate the organization of clips into folders based on their content or metadata. For instance, clips containing financial data can be automatically moved to a "Finance" folder.

- Notifications and Alerts: Set up automated notifications and alerts for specific actions, such as when a clip is updated or when a new clip is added to a shared folder. This keeps team members informed and ensures timely responses.

- Integration with Microsoft 365: Create automated workflows that interact with other Microsoft 365 tools. For example, an automation rule could be set to create a task in Microsoft To Do whenever a new clip is added to a project folder in ClipCharm.

Customizing the User Interface

Personalizing the Workspace

Customizing the user interface is an essential part of optimizing the ClipCharm experience. Users can personalize their workspace to align with their preferences and workflow needs.

- Theme and Appearance: Users can choose from different themes and color schemes to customize the appearance of ClipCharm. This includes selecting light or dark mode, adjusting font sizes, and configuring layout options.

- Dashboard Configuration: Users can configure their dashboard to display widgets and shortcuts that are most relevant to their work. For example, a user may choose to add a widget that shows recent clips, upcoming deadlines, or frequently used tools.

Custom Layouts

Creating custom layouts allows users to arrange their workspace in a way that enhances their productivity.

- Drag-and-Drop Functionality: ClipCharm supports drag-and-drop functionality for arranging panels, widgets, and toolbars. Users can move elements around to create a layout that suits their workflow.

- Saving Layouts: Custom layouts can be saved and applied across different devices or sessions. This ensures that users maintain a consistent experience regardless of where they access ClipCharm.

Custom Templates and Clip Types

Creating and Managing Custom Templates

Custom templates are an excellent way to standardize content and streamline the creation process for frequently used clip types.

- Designing Templates: Users can create custom templates for various clip types, including text, images, and multimedia. Templates can include predefined fields, formatting, and placeholders to simplify content creation.

- Template Management: Custom templates can be managed through a dedicated interface where users can edit, delete, or duplicate existing templates. This interface also allows users to categorize templates for easy access.

Defining Clip Types

Defining custom clip types helps organize and classify content according to specific needs.

- Creating Clip Types: Users can create custom clip types based on their requirements. For example, clip types could include "Meeting Notes," "Project Updates," or "Research Findings."

- Customizing Clip Fields: Each clip type can have customized fields and attributes that capture relevant information. For instance, a "Project Update" clip type might include fields for project status, deadlines, and team members involved.

Advanced Integration Settings

Integrating with External Applications

Advanced integration settings allow ClipCharm to interact with external applications and services beyond Microsoft 365.

- Configuring APIs: Users can configure API integrations to connect ClipCharm with other applications, such as CRM systems, project management tools, or custom business applications. This enables seamless data exchange and workflow automation.

- Custom Webhooks: Webhooks can be configured to trigger actions in external systems based on events in ClipCharm. For example, a webhook could be set up to notify a third-party application whenever a clip is updated or a new clip is created.

Synchronizing Data Across Platforms

Data synchronization ensures that information in ClipCharm remains consistent across different platforms and devices.

- Setting Up Sync Options: Users can configure synchronization settings to ensure that data is updated in real-time across all devices and applications. This includes syncing clips, templates, and user settings.

- Managing Sync Conflicts: In cases where data conflicts arise, ClipCharm provides tools to manage and resolve synchronization issues. Users can review conflict logs and choose the appropriate action to reconcile discrepancies.

Security and Privacy Settings

Configuring Security Settings

Ensuring the security and privacy of data in ClipCharm is essential, especially in environments where sensitive information is handled.

- Setting Up Encryption: Users can configure encryption settings to protect data at rest and in transit. This includes enabling SSL/TLS for secure communications and applying encryption to stored clips.

- Access Control: Advanced access control settings allow users to define who can access and modify specific clips or folders. This includes setting up role-based access controls and applying security policies.

Privacy Options

Privacy settings help manage how user data is collected and used.

- Data Collection Preferences: Users can configure preferences for data collection and usage, such as opting in or out of telemetry data sharing.

- Managing Personal Information: Privacy settings also include options for managing personal information, such as profile details and activity logs.

Conclusion

Advanced configuration options in ClipCharm provide users with powerful tools to tailor the application to their specific needs and preferences. By leveraging these options, users can enhance their productivity, streamline their workflows, and ensure that ClipCharm integrates seamlessly with their existing systems. Whether through advanced automation, customized user interfaces, or secure data management, these features empower users to make the most of their ClipCharm experience within the Microsoft 365 ecosystem.

CHAPTER V
Best Practices for Using ClipCharm

5.1 Organizing Your Clips Efficiently

Organizing your clips efficiently is crucial for maximizing productivity and ensuring easy access to your content. Proper organization helps prevent the frustration of searching for misplaced clips and allows for seamless collaboration with team members. In this section, we will explore effective strategies for organizing your clips, starting with the importance of naming conventions.

5.1.1 Naming Conventions

Naming conventions are a standardized way of naming your clips to ensure consistency, clarity, and ease of retrieval. By adopting a systematic approach to naming your clips, you can significantly reduce the time spent searching for specific items and improve overall workflow efficiency. Here are several key aspects to consider when developing and implementing naming conventions for your ClipCharm clips.

1. Consistency

Consistency is the cornerstone of effective naming conventions. Ensure that everyone in your organization follows the same naming rules to avoid confusion and maintain order. This can be achieved by creating a comprehensive naming convention guide that outlines the rules and examples for different types of clips. Consistency makes it easier for team members to understand and use the system, leading to a more organized and efficient workflow.

2. Descriptive Names

Use descriptive names that clearly indicate the content and purpose of the clip. Avoid vague or generic terms that do not provide enough information about the clip. Descriptive names should include key details such as the subject, date, and version number. For example, instead of naming a clip "Meeting Notes," you could use "Team_Meeting_Notes_2024-07-29_v1." This provides a clear indication of the content, date, and version, making it easier to identify and locate the clip later.

3. Use of Dates

Incorporating dates into your naming conventions can be extremely helpful for tracking the chronology of your clips. Use a consistent date format, such as YYYY-MM-DD, to ensure clarity and avoid confusion. Placing the date at the beginning or end of the clip name can help you quickly identify the most recent version or the specific timeframe of the content. For example, "Project_Update_2024-07-29" is more informative than simply "Project_Update."

4. Version Control

Version control is essential for managing updates and revisions to your clips. Including a version number in the clip name allows you to keep track of changes and ensures that team members are working with the most up-to-date information. Adopt a consistent format for versioning, such as "v1," "v2," "v3," etc., and update the version number each time a significant change is made to the clip. For example, "Marketing_Plan_v1" can be updated to "Marketing_Plan_v2" after revisions.

5. Abbreviations and Acronyms

While using abbreviations and acronyms can save time, it is important to ensure they are easily understood by all team members. Create a standardized list of commonly used abbreviations and acronyms within your organization and include it in your naming convention guide. This list should be accessible to all team members to avoid confusion and maintain consistency. For example, "Q1_Report_2024" is clear if "Q1" is commonly understood to mean "First Quarter."

6. Avoid Special Characters

Special characters such as slashes, colons, and asterisks can cause issues with file systems and software applications. To avoid potential problems, use only alphanumeric characters, underscores, and hyphens in your clip names. For example, instead of "Sales/Report: Q12024," use "Sales_Report_Q1_2024."

7. Length and Readability

While it is important to be descriptive, avoid making clip names excessively long. Long names can be difficult to read and may be truncated in some applications, making them less useful. Aim for a balance between descriptiveness and brevity. For example, "Annual_Financial_Report_2024_Summary" is more readable than "Summary_of_the_Annual_Financial_Report_for_the_Year_2024."

8. Examples of Effective Naming Conventions

To illustrate the principles discussed, here are a few examples of effective naming conventions:

- Meeting Notes:

  - "Team_Meeting_Notes_2024-07-29_v1"

  - "Client_Meeting_Notes_2024-07-30_v2"

- Project Files:

  - "Project_Alpha_Plan_2024-07-29_v1"

  - "Project_Beta_Report_2024-08-01_v3"

- Marketing Materials:

  - "Marketing_Strategy_Q3_2024_v1"

  - "Ad_Campaign_Summer_2024_v2"

- Financial Documents:

  - "Q1_Financial_Report_2024_v1"

- "Annual_Budget_2024_v2"

9. Implementing Naming Conventions

Implementing naming conventions requires clear communication and training within your organization. Here are steps to effectively implement naming conventions:

1. Develop a Naming Convention Guide:

  - Create a detailed guide that outlines the naming rules, provides examples, and explains the rationale behind the conventions.

2. Communicate the Conventions:

  - Share the guide with all team members and ensure they understand the importance of following the conventions.

3. Training and Workshops:

  - Conduct training sessions and workshops to demonstrate the naming conventions and address any questions or concerns.

4. Monitor Compliance:

  - Regularly review and monitor the usage of naming conventions to ensure compliance and address any deviations.

5. Feedback and Improvement:

  - Encourage feedback from team members and make improvements to the naming conventions as needed.

10. Benefits of Effective Naming Conventions

Adopting effective naming conventions offers several benefits:

- Improved Organization:

  - Consistent and descriptive names make it easier to organize and locate clips, reducing the time spent searching for specific items.

- Enhanced Collaboration:

 - Clear and consistent naming conventions facilitate collaboration by ensuring that all team members can easily understand and use the clips.

- Version Control:

 - Including version numbers helps track changes and ensures that everyone is working with the most up-to-date information.

- Reduced Errors:

 - Avoiding special characters and maintaining readability minimizes the risk of errors and issues with file systems and applications.

- Professionalism:

 - Well-organized and clearly named clips reflect a professional approach to content management, enhancing the overall efficiency and effectiveness of your organization.

In conclusion, naming conventions are a fundamental aspect of organizing your clips efficiently. By adopting consistent, descriptive, and clear naming conventions, you can improve productivity, enhance collaboration, and maintain a well-organized clip library. Implement these best practices in your ClipCharm workflow to maximize the benefits and ensure a streamlined and efficient content management system.

5.1.2 Categorization and Tagging

Effective categorization and tagging of your clips in ClipCharm is essential for maintaining an organized and efficient clip library. As you accumulate a large number of clips, the ability to quickly locate and retrieve the right clip becomes crucial. This section will guide you through the best practices for categorizing and tagging your clips, ensuring that your library remains manageable and accessible.

Understanding Categorization and Tagging

Categorization and tagging are methods of organizing content to improve searchability and retrieval. Categorization involves grouping clips into predefined categories, while tagging allows you to attach descriptive labels to each clip. Together, these methods help you create a structured and easily navigable clip library.

Benefits of Categorization and Tagging

1. Enhanced Searchability: By categorizing and tagging your clips, you make it easier to find specific clips using search functions.

2. Improved Organization: Grouping similar clips together helps maintain a clean and organized library.

3. Efficient Retrieval: Tags enable quick retrieval of clips based on specific attributes or keywords.

4. Better Collaboration: Consistent categorization and tagging facilitate collaboration by ensuring all team members can easily find and use clips.

Setting Up Categories

Categories are broad groups that help you organize your clips by general themes or topics. Setting up categories requires a clear understanding of the types of clips you create and their intended use.

Steps to Create Effective Categories

1. Identify Main Themes: Start by identifying the main themes or topics relevant to your work. These themes will form the basis of your categories. For example, if you are creating clips for marketing, categories could include "Social Media," "Email Campaigns," "Product Launches," etc.

2. Define Categories Clearly: Ensure that each category has a clear and specific definition to avoid overlap. For instance, "Social Media" should include all clips related to social media platforms and strategies, while "Email Campaigns" should focus solely on email marketing content.

3. Limit the Number of Categories: Too many categories can be overwhelming and counterproductive. Aim to create a manageable number of categories that cover all your main themes without becoming overly granular.

4. Review and Adjust: Periodically review your categories to ensure they remain relevant and useful. As your library grows, you may need to add, merge, or rename categories.

Example Categories

Here are some example categories for different use cases:

- *Marketing Clips:*

  - Social Media

  - Email Campaigns

  - Product Launches

  - Advertisements

  - Market Research

- *Educational Clips:*

  - Tutorials

  - Lectures

  - Webinars

  - Demonstrations

  - Interviews

- *Project Management Clips:*

  - Planning

  - Meetings

  - Reports

  - Deliverables

- Feedback

Implementing Tags

Tags are more specific than categories and allow for detailed labeling of clips based on attributes, keywords, or topics. Tags provide an additional layer of organization, making it easier to locate clips that share common attributes across different categories.

Best Practices for Tagging

1. Be Specific and Descriptive: Use specific and descriptive tags to accurately label your clips. For example, instead of a generic tag like "Video," use tags like "Tutorial Video," "Marketing Video," or "Training Video."

2. Use Consistent Terminology: Consistency is key to effective tagging. Establish a standardized set of tags and ensure all team members use the same terminology. This prevents confusion and redundancy.

3. Limit the Number of Tags: While it's tempting to add numerous tags to a clip, limit the number of tags to those that are most relevant. Over-tagging can clutter your library and make it difficult to identify the most important attributes.

4. Combine Tags for Precision: Combine multiple tags to create a precise and detailed description of a clip. For example, a clip could be tagged with "Social Media," "Instagram," and "Ad Campaign" to indicate that it is an Instagram ad campaign clip related to social media marketing.

Example Tags

Here are some example tags for different scenarios:

- *Marketing Clips:*

  - Campaign

  - Social Media

  - Instagram

- Facebook

- Ad Campaign

- SEO

- Content Marketing

- *Educational Clips:*

  - Tutorial

  - Lecture

  - Webinar

  - Online Course

  - Interview

  - Demonstration

- *Project Management Clips:*

  - Meeting

  - Planning

  - Report

  - Feedback

  - Deadline

Combining Categories and Tags

The combination of categories and tags provides a powerful organization system for your clip library. Categories offer a broad structure, while tags add specificity and detail. Together, they ensure that your clips are easy to find and use.

Example Scenario

Imagine you have a clip library for a marketing department. You might have the following setup:

- Categories:

  - Social Media

  - Email Campaigns

  - Product Launches

  - Advertisements

  - Market Research

- Tags:

  - Campaign

  - Instagram

  - Facebook

  - Ad Campaign

  - Video

  - Image

  - SEO

  - Content Marketing

A clip related to an Instagram ad campaign could be categorized under "Social Media" and tagged with "Instagram," "Ad Campaign," and "Video." This setup allows you to find the clip easily by browsing the "Social Media" category or by searching for any of the tags.

Implementing Categorization and Tagging in ClipCharm

ClipCharm provides intuitive tools for categorizing and tagging clips. Here's how to effectively implement these practices within ClipCharm.

Creating Categories in ClipCharm

1. Access the Categories Section: Navigate to the ClipCharm dashboard and access the categories section from the main menu.

2. Add New Categories: Click on "Add Category" and enter the name and description of the new category.

3. Assign Clips to Categories: When creating or editing a clip, select the appropriate category from the dropdown menu. Ensure that each clip is assigned to the most relevant category.

Adding Tags to Clips in ClipCharm

1. Access the Tagging Section: When creating or editing a clip, locate the tagging section in the clip settings.

2. Enter Relevant Tags: Enter relevant tags for the clip. Use commas to separate multiple tags.

3. Save and Apply Tags: Save the changes to apply the tags to the clip. The tags will now be associated with the clip and can be used for searching and filtering.

Utilizing Categories and Tags for Efficient Search and Retrieval

Once your clips are categorized and tagged, you can leverage ClipCharm's search and filter features to efficiently locate and retrieve clips.

Searching by Category

1. Navigate to the Search Bar: Use the search bar at the top of the ClipCharm dashboard.

2. Select Category Filter: Choose the category filter and select the desired category from the dropdown menu.

3. Enter Search Keywords: Enter relevant keywords to further refine your search within the selected category.

4. Review Search Results: Browse the search results to find the desired clip.

Searching by Tag

1. Navigate to the Search Bar: Use the search bar at the top of the ClipCharm dashboard.

2. Select Tag Filter: Choose the tag filter and enter the desired tag(s).

3. Combine Multiple Tags: Combine multiple tags for a more precise search.

4. Review Search Results: Browse the search results to find the desired clip.

Using Combined Search

1. Navigate to the Search Bar: Use the search bar at the top of the ClipCharm dashboard.

2. Select Category and Tag Filters: Choose both category and tag filters to refine your search.

3. Enter Search Keywords: Enter relevant keywords for a highly targeted search.

4. Review Search Results: Browse the search results to find the desired clip.

Maintaining Consistency in Categorization and Tagging

Maintaining consistency in categorization and tagging is crucial for the long-term efficiency of your clip library.

Establishing Guidelines

1. Create a Tagging Policy: Develop a tagging policy that outlines the standard tags and categories to be used.

2. Educate Team Members: Ensure all team members are aware of the tagging policy and understand the importance of consistent tagging.

3. Regular Reviews: Periodically review the categorization and tagging system to ensure it remains effective and relevant.

Monitoring and Adjusting

1. Track Usage and Feedback: Monitor how clips are being categorized and tagged. Gather feedback from team members to identify any issues or areas for improvement.

2. Make Adjustments: Adjust categories and tags as needed to accommodate new types of clips or changes in workflows.

3. Update Guidelines: Update the tagging policy and guidelines based on feedback and adjustments.

Conclusion

Effective categorization and tagging of clips in ClipCharm are fundamental to maintaining an organized and efficient clip library. By following the best practices outlined in this section, you can ensure that your clips are easily searchable, retrievable, and usable. This organization not only enhances your productivity but also fosters better collaboration within your team, making ClipCharm an invaluable tool in your Microsoft 365 toolkit.

5.2 Enhancing Collaboration with ClipCharm

Collaboration is key in today's fast-paced work environments, and ClipCharm offers a range of features to enhance teamwork and ensure smooth, efficient workflows. This chapter focuses on how ClipCharm can be used to facilitate collaboration, with a particular emphasis on effective sharing strategies.

5.2.1 Effective Sharing Strategies

Sharing content effectively is crucial for collaborative work. ClipCharm provides several tools and methods to ensure that your clips reach the right people at the right time. Here are some strategies to make the most out of ClipCharm's sharing capabilities.

Understanding Sharing Permissions

One of the first steps in sharing clips effectively is understanding the permissions settings within ClipCharm. Permissions dictate who can view, edit, and share your clips. Here's a breakdown of the different permission levels:

- Viewer: Can only view the clip.

- Editor: Can view and edit the clip.

- Owner: Can view, edit, and manage permissions.

By setting the appropriate permissions, you can control access and ensure that only authorized personnel can make changes.

Sharing via Email

Email remains a powerful tool for sharing clips within an organization. ClipCharm integrates seamlessly with Microsoft 365's Outlook, allowing users to share clips directly through email. Here's how you can do it effectively:

1. Compose a New Email: Open Outlook and start a new email.

2. Attach the Clip: Click on the ClipCharm icon within the Outlook toolbar to attach a clip directly from your ClipCharm library.

3. Add Recipients: Add the recipients who need access to the clip.

4. Set Permissions: Before sending, ensure that you have set the correct permissions for each recipient.

5. Include a Message: Provide context or instructions in the body of the email to guide the recipients on what is expected.

Using Shared Workspaces

ClipCharm's shared workspaces allow teams to collaborate on clips in a centralized location. Shared workspaces are particularly useful for projects that require input from multiple team members. Here's how to use shared workspaces effectively:

1. Create a Shared Workspace: Navigate to the ClipCharm dashboard and select 'Create Workspace'.

2. Invite Team Members: Add team members to the workspace by entering their email addresses.

3. Organize Clips: Use folders and tags to organize clips within the workspace for easy access.

4. Set Roles: Assign roles (Viewer, Editor, Owner) to each team member based on their responsibilities.

Shared workspaces facilitate real-time collaboration, ensuring that all team members have the latest information and can contribute effectively.

Leveraging Microsoft Teams Integration

Microsoft Teams is a powerful collaboration tool, and its integration with ClipCharm enhances the sharing experience. Here's how to leverage this integration:

1. Add ClipCharm to Teams: Go to the Teams app store, search for ClipCharm, and add it to your Teams workspace.

2. Share Clips in Channels: Post clips directly in Teams channels where relevant discussions are taking place. Use the ClipCharm tab to attach clips.

3. Collaborate in Real-Time: Team members can view, edit, and discuss clips in real-time within Teams, streamlining the workflow.

4. Notifications: Enable notifications to keep team members informed about updates to shared clips.

Using Shareable Links

Shareable links are another efficient way to distribute clips to a wider audience, including those outside your organization. ClipCharm allows you to generate shareable links with customizable permissions. Here's how to use them:

1. Generate a Link: Select the clip you want to share and click on the 'Share' button to generate a link.

2. Customize Permissions: Choose whether the link should allow viewing only, or if editing and sharing should be permitted.

3. Set Expiry Dates: For added security, set an expiry date for the link, ensuring it's only accessible for a specific period.

4. Distribute the Link: Copy the link and share it via email, chat, or any other communication platform.

Embedding Clips

For seamless integration into presentations, reports, or websites, ClipCharm allows clips to be embedded directly into other documents. Here's how to do it:

1. Copy Embed Code: Select the clip and click on the 'Embed' option to generate an embed code.

2. Paste into Document: Paste the embed code into your document, website, or presentation where you want the clip to appear.

3. Adjust Settings: Customize the embed settings to control the appearance and functionality of the embedded clip.

Embedding clips ensures that content is easily accessible without the need to switch between applications.

Best Practices for Effective Sharing

To maximize the effectiveness of your sharing strategies, consider the following best practices:

- Clear Communication: Always provide context and instructions when sharing clips to ensure recipients understand the purpose and required actions.

- Regular Updates: Keep shared clips and workspaces updated to ensure all collaborators have access to the latest information.

- Feedback Mechanisms: Encourage feedback from team members on shared clips to improve the quality and relevance of the content.

- Security: Be mindful of security settings and permissions to protect sensitive information.

By implementing these strategies and utilizing ClipCharm's robust sharing features, you can significantly enhance collaboration within your team and organization. Effective sharing not only improves productivity but also fosters a more connected and efficient working environment.

5.2.2 Real-Time Collaboration Tips

Real-time collaboration is an essential feature in modern workflows, allowing teams to work together seamlessly, regardless of their physical location. ClipCharm, integrated within Microsoft 365, offers a range of functionalities that enhance real-time collaboration, making it easier for teams to create, share, and refine content collectively. This section will delve into practical tips and strategies for leveraging ClipCharm to its fullest potential in real-time collaborative environments.

Understanding Real-Time Collaboration in ClipCharm

Before diving into the tips, it is crucial to understand what real-time collaboration entails in the context of ClipCharm. Real-time collaboration means multiple users can simultaneously access, edit, and comment on clips and projects within ClipCharm. Changes are visible to all collaborators instantly, fostering a dynamic and interactive work environment.

Setting Up for Successful Real-Time Collaboration

To ensure effective real-time collaboration, the initial setup is crucial. Here are some steps to set up your ClipCharm environment for optimal collaboration:

1. Ensure Everyone Has Access:

 - Ensure that all team members have access to ClipCharm and the necessary permissions to edit and collaborate on clips. This might involve adding users to your ClipCharm workspace or granting specific access rights.

2. Standardize Your Tools:

 - Ensure that all team members are using compatible versions of ClipCharm and Microsoft 365 applications. Compatibility issues can hinder collaboration and lead to frustration.

3. Establish Clear Communication Channels:

 - Use Microsoft Teams, which integrates seamlessly with ClipCharm, for communication. Create specific channels for different projects to keep discussions organized and focused.

Tips for Effective Real-Time Collaboration

1. Leverage Shared Workspaces:

 - Utilize shared workspaces within ClipCharm where team members can access and contribute to projects. Shared workspaces ensure that everyone is working on the most up-to-date versions of clips and can see changes as they happen.

2. Define Roles and Responsibilities:

 - Clearly define the roles and responsibilities of each team member in the collaborative process. This can include assigning specific tasks or sections of a project to different individuals, ensuring accountability and clarity.

3. Use Commenting and Annotation Tools:

 - ClipCharm offers robust commenting and annotation tools that allow team members to provide feedback directly on the clips. Encourage the use of these tools to discuss changes, suggest improvements, and highlight important points.

4. Implement Version Control:

 - Use ClipCharm's version control features to track changes and revert to previous versions if necessary. This helps maintain a clear record of edits and ensures that no valuable work is lost.

5. Conduct Regular Sync-Up Meetings:

 - Schedule regular meetings to sync up with the team, discuss progress, address any issues, and plan the next steps. These meetings can be conducted via Microsoft Teams, ensuring all team members are aligned and any roadblocks are addressed promptly.

Practical Collaboration Scenarios

To illustrate the application of these tips, let's explore some practical scenarios where ClipCharm can be utilized for real-time collaboration.

Scenario 1: Collaborative Content Creation

In this scenario, a marketing team is working on a series of promotional videos. Using ClipCharm, they can:

1. Create a Shared Project Workspace:

 - The project manager sets up a shared workspace in ClipCharm where all team members can access the video clips, scripts, and related materials.

2. Assign Roles:

 - The video editor is responsible for assembling the clips, the content writer for drafting the script, and the graphic designer for adding visual elements.

3. Real-Time Editing and Feedback:

- As the video editor assembles the clips, the content writer can simultaneously refine the script. Using ClipCharm's annotation tools, the graphic designer can suggest where to insert graphics or text overlays.

4. Using Comments for Feedback:

- Team members use the commenting feature to provide feedback on specific sections of the video. For example, the project manager might comment on the pacing of a particular scene, while the graphic designer suggests adjustments to the visual style.

Scenario 2: Research and Development Collaboration

A research team is working on a new product prototype. ClipCharm facilitates their collaboration as follows:

1. Documenting the Research Process:

- Researchers create and share clips documenting their findings, experimental setups, and results. Each clip is accessible to all team members, ensuring transparency and collective input.

2. Real-Time Data Analysis:

- Data analysts can upload and annotate charts, graphs, and statistical data in ClipCharm. Researchers can view these annotations and provide instant feedback or additional data.

3. Collaborative Problem Solving:

- During a live brainstorming session on Microsoft Teams, team members can simultaneously edit a shared ClipCharm project. This allows them to integrate ideas in real time and refine the prototype collaboratively.

Scenario 3: Educational Collaboration

In an educational setting, teachers and students can use ClipCharm for group projects:

1. Creating Group Workspaces:

- Teachers set up group workspaces where students can upload and edit their project clips. Each group has a dedicated space, fostering a collaborative environment.

2. Real-Time Peer Review:

 - Students use ClipCharm to review each other's work, providing constructive feedback through comments and annotations. This peer review process helps improve the quality of the projects.

3. Instructor Feedback:

 - Teachers can monitor progress in real time, offering guidance and feedback at various stages of the project. This immediate support helps keep students on track and addresses any issues promptly.

Best Practices for Maintaining Momentum

Maintaining momentum in a real-time collaborative environment requires consistent effort and effective management. Here are some best practices to ensure ongoing success:

1. Regular Updates and Check-Ins:

 - Schedule regular check-ins to discuss progress, address challenges, and celebrate milestones. These check-ins can be brief but are crucial for maintaining engagement and momentum.

2. Encourage Open Communication:

 - Foster a culture of open communication where team members feel comfortable sharing ideas, concerns, and feedback. This openness is essential for a healthy collaborative environment.

3. Provide Training and Support:

 - Ensure that all team members are comfortable using ClipCharm and understand its features. Provide training sessions or resources to help them get up to speed.

4. Recognize and Celebrate Contributions:

 - Acknowledge and celebrate the contributions of team members. Recognition can be a powerful motivator and helps build a positive team culture.

5. Continuously Improve Processes:

- Regularly review and refine your collaboration processes. Seek feedback from the team on what's working well and where there's room for improvement.

Conclusion

Real-time collaboration using ClipCharm in Microsoft 365 can significantly enhance productivity, creativity, and team cohesion. By leveraging shared workspaces, defining clear roles, utilizing commenting and annotation tools, implementing version control, and conducting regular sync-up meetings, teams can work together more effectively and efficiently. Practical scenarios demonstrate how these strategies can be applied in various contexts, from marketing and research to education.

Maintaining momentum through regular updates, open communication, training, recognition, and continuous improvement ensures sustained success in real-time collaborative efforts. With these tips and best practices, your team can maximize the benefits of ClipCharm and achieve remarkable results in your collaborative projects.

5.3 Maintaining and Updating Your Clip Library

Proper maintenance and regular updates to your ClipCharm library are essential to ensure that your clips remain organized, relevant, and readily accessible. This section will guide you through the best practices for maintaining and updating your clip library.

5.3.1 Regular Maintenance Tasks

Regular maintenance of your ClipCharm library involves a series of routine tasks designed to keep your clips organized and up-to-date. By performing these tasks periodically, you can ensure that your clip library remains efficient and useful. Below, we will discuss several key maintenance tasks and how to perform them effectively.

1. Review and Update Clip Content

Periodically review the content of your clips to ensure that they remain relevant and accurate. This involves checking for outdated information, correcting any errors, and updating clips to reflect the latest data or trends. Here are some steps to follow:

- Schedule Regular Reviews: Set a schedule for reviewing your clips. Depending on the nature of your content, this could be monthly, quarterly, or annually. Regular reviews help catch outdated or incorrect information before it becomes problematic.

- Check for Relevance: Ensure that the content of each clip is still relevant to your audience. Remove or update clips that no longer serve a useful purpose.

- Update Information: If there are changes in the information presented in your clips, update them accordingly. This could involve adding new data, correcting inaccuracies, or revising content to reflect new developments.

- Validate Sources: Ensure that the sources of your information are still reliable and up-to-date. Replace outdated sources with current, credible references.

2. Organize Your Clips

Keeping your clips well-organized makes it easier to find and use them when needed. An organized clip library also helps improve efficiency and productivity. Here are some tips for organizing your clips:

- Create Folders and Subfolders: Use folders and subfolders to categorize your clips by topic, project, or any other relevant criteria. This helps in quickly locating the clips you need.

- Use Descriptive Names: Give your clips descriptive names that clearly indicate their content. Avoid using vague or generic names that make it difficult to identify the clip's purpose.

- Implement Tagging System: Utilize a tagging system to label your clips with keywords that describe their content. This allows for easy searching and filtering of clips.

- Archive Old Clips: Move outdated or rarely used clips to an archive folder. This keeps your main library clutter-free while still retaining the clips for future reference if needed.

3. Backup Your Clip Library

Regularly backing up your clip library is crucial to prevent data loss due to accidental deletion, system failures, or other unforeseen events. Here's how to ensure your clips are safely backed up:

- Use Cloud Storage: Store your clips in a cloud storage service such as OneDrive, Google Drive, or Dropbox. Cloud storage provides automatic backups and easy access from any device.

- Schedule Regular Backups: Set up automatic backups at regular intervals to ensure that your clips are always up-to-date. Daily or weekly backups are recommended, depending on how frequently you update your clips.

- Maintain Local Copies: In addition to cloud storage, keep local copies of your clips on your computer or an external hard drive. This provides an extra layer of security in case of internet outages or issues with cloud services.

4. Perform Cleanup and Deletion

Regularly cleaning up your clip library helps maintain its efficiency and prevents clutter. This involves deleting unnecessary clips and organizing remaining ones. Here are some steps for performing cleanup:

- Identify Redundant Clips: Look for duplicate or similar clips and consolidate them into a single clip. This reduces redundancy and saves storage space.

- Delete Unnecessary Clips: Remove clips that are no longer needed or relevant. This includes outdated clips, test clips, or any content that doesn't serve a clear purpose.

- Clear Temporary Files: Delete any temporary files or drafts that were created during the clip creation process but are no longer needed.

5. Monitor Clip Usage and Performance

Keeping track of how your clips are used and their performance can provide valuable insights for maintaining and improving your clip library. Here's how to monitor clip usage effectively:

- Track Access and Views: Use analytics tools to track how often your clips are accessed and viewed. This helps identify popular clips and those that may need improvement or updates.

- Gather User Feedback: Solicit feedback from users who access your clips. This can provide insights into how the clips are being used and any areas for improvement.

- Analyze Engagement Metrics: Look at metrics such as view duration, click-through rates, and engagement levels to assess the effectiveness of your clips.

6. Optimize Clip Storage

Efficient storage management ensures that your clips are easily accessible and that your storage space is used optimally. Here are some tips for optimizing clip storage:

- Compress Large Files: Use file compression tools to reduce the size of large clips without compromising quality. This saves storage space and speeds up file transfer.

- Use Consistent File Formats: Standardize the file formats for your clips to ensure compatibility and ease of use. Common formats include MP4 for videos and PDF for documents.

- Implement Version Control: Use version control systems to manage different versions of your clips. This helps keep track of changes and allows you to revert to previous versions if needed.

7. Regularly Update Software and Tools

Keeping your ClipCharm software and related tools up-to-date ensures that you have access to the latest features and improvements. Here's how to stay current with updates:

- Enable Automatic Updates: Turn on automatic updates for ClipCharm and any related software tools. This ensures that you always have the latest versions installed.

- Check for Updates Manually: Periodically check for software updates manually to ensure you haven't missed any important updates.

- Review Release Notes: Read the release notes for updates to understand what changes or improvements have been made. This helps you make the most of new features and enhancements.

8. Conduct Training and Skill Development

Regular training and skill development ensure that you and your team are proficient in using ClipCharm and can take full advantage of its features. Here are some ways to enhance your skills:

- Attend Webinars and Workshops: Participate in webinars, workshops, and training sessions offered by ClipCharm or third-party providers. These sessions often cover new features, best practices, and advanced techniques.

- Access Online Tutorials: Use online tutorials and courses to learn new skills and improve your proficiency with ClipCharm. Many resources are available for free or at a low cost.

- Practice Regularly: Regular practice is key to mastering any tool. Set aside time to explore and experiment with different features of ClipCharm.

9. Set Up a Maintenance Schedule

Establishing a regular maintenance schedule helps ensure that all the above tasks are performed consistently and efficiently. Here's how to set up an effective maintenance schedule:

- Define Maintenance Tasks: List all the maintenance tasks that need to be performed regularly, such as reviewing clips, organizing the library, and backing up data.

- Assign Responsibilities: Assign specific tasks to team members or designate a maintenance manager to oversee the entire process.

- Create a Calendar: Use a calendar or task management tool to schedule maintenance tasks. Set reminders and deadlines to ensure tasks are completed on time.

- Conduct Regular Reviews: Periodically review your maintenance schedule to ensure it is effective and make adjustments as needed.

10. Develop a Maintenance Checklist

A maintenance checklist serves as a handy reference to ensure that all necessary tasks are performed during each maintenance session. Here's how to create a comprehensive checklist:

- List All Tasks: Include all regular maintenance tasks in the checklist, along with any specific steps or sub-tasks.

- Prioritize Tasks: Prioritize tasks based on their importance and frequency. This helps ensure that critical tasks are always completed.

- Include Documentation: Provide detailed instructions for each task, including any relevant screenshots or examples.

- Update Regularly: Review and update the checklist regularly to reflect any changes in your maintenance processes or new tasks that need to be added.

11. Conduct Periodic Audits

Periodic audits of your clip library help ensure that your maintenance efforts are effective and that your library remains in good condition. Here's how to conduct a successful audit:

- Review Clip Quality: Assess the overall quality of your clips, including their content, organization, and relevance.

- Evaluate Efficiency: Check how efficiently your clip library is being used, including ease of access, searchability, and user satisfaction.

- Identify Areas for Improvement: Look for any areas where your maintenance processes can be improved or streamlined.

- Document Findings: Record the results of your audit, including any issues identified and recommendations for improvement.

By following these regular maintenance tasks, you can ensure that your ClipCharm library remains organized, relevant, and efficient. Regular maintenance not only improves the usability of your clips but also enhances the overall productivity and effectiveness of your team.

5.3.2 Keeping Your Clips Up-to-Date

Keeping your ClipCharm clips up-to-date is crucial for maintaining an efficient and effective clip library. An up-to-date clip library ensures that the information you share with your team is current, relevant, and useful. This section will cover several strategies and best practices for keeping your clips up-to-date, including regular reviews, utilizing version control, and leveraging ClipCharm's features for efficient updates.

1. Schedule Regular Reviews

One of the most effective ways to keep your clips up-to-date is to schedule regular reviews of your clip library. This can be done monthly, quarterly, or at any interval that suits your workflow. During these reviews, check each clip for accuracy and relevance. Remove outdated information and update any clips that have changed due to new information, policies, or procedures.

2. Implement Version Control

Version control is a systematic approach to managing changes in your clips over time. By keeping track of different versions of a clip, you can ensure that the most recent and accurate version is always available while maintaining a history of changes. This can be particularly useful when multiple team members are collaborating on clip content.

To implement version control in ClipCharm:

- Create a Naming Convention for Versions: Include version numbers or dates in your clip names to easily identify the latest version. For example, use names like "ProjectPlan_v1" or "ProjectPlan_2024_07_01".

- Use Version Comments: When updating a clip, add a comment summarizing the changes made. This helps team members understand what has changed and why.

- Archive Old Versions: Instead of deleting old versions, archive them. This allows you to refer back to previous versions if needed.

3. Leverage ClipCharm's Update Features

ClipCharm offers several features that can help streamline the process of keeping your clips up-to-date. These features include:

- Automated Alerts: Set up automated alerts to notify you when a clip has not been updated in a specified period. This can help you remember to review and update clips regularly.

- Change Tracking: Use ClipCharm's change tracking feature to monitor modifications made to clips. This allows you to see who made changes, what changes were made, and when they were made.

- Templates: Use templates for common clip types. When updates are needed, you can modify the template, and all clips based on that template will be automatically updated.

4. Collaborate with Your Team

Effective collaboration with your team can significantly improve the accuracy and relevance of your clips. Encourage team members to contribute to the clip update process by:

- Assigning Roles: Designate team members as clip owners responsible for specific clips or categories. These owners will be responsible for ensuring their clips are up-to-date.

- Feedback Mechanisms: Create a feedback loop where team members can suggest updates or report outdated information. This can be done through comments on clips or a shared feedback document.

- Regular Meetings: Hold regular meetings to discuss clip content and identify areas that need updating. This collaborative approach ensures that all team members are aware of changes and can provide input.

5. Use a Centralized Clip Repository

Maintaining a centralized clip repository can make it easier to manage and update your clips. This repository should be accessible to all team members and should be the single source of truth for your clip library. In Microsoft 365, you can use SharePoint or OneDrive to create a centralized repository.

- SharePoint: Create a SharePoint site dedicated to your clip library. Use document libraries to organize clips by category and implement version control and permissions to manage access.

- OneDrive: Use OneDrive to store and share clips with your team. Organize clips into folders and use sharing settings to control access and editing permissions.

6. Regular Training and Updates

Ensure that all team members are trained on the importance of keeping clips up-to-date and how to do so. Provide regular training sessions and updates to keep everyone informed about best practices and new features in ClipCharm.

- Training Sessions: Conduct training sessions to teach team members how to update clips, use version control, and collaborate effectively.

- Update Communications: Send regular communications, such as newsletters or email updates, to inform team members about changes to clip content, new features in ClipCharm, and best practices for maintaining the clip library.

7. Monitor Clip Usage and Engagement

Monitoring clip usage and engagement can help you identify which clips are most frequently used and which ones may need updates. ClipCharm provides analytics tools to track clip views, shares, and feedback.

- View Analytics: Use ClipCharm's analytics to monitor how often clips are viewed and by whom. High view counts indicate that a clip is valuable and may need regular updates to stay relevant.

- Feedback and Ratings: Enable feedback and rating features on clips. This allows team members to provide input on the accuracy and usefulness of clips, helping you identify clips that need updates.

8. Create an Update Schedule

Establish a regular update schedule for your clip library. This schedule should outline when reviews and updates will take place and who is responsible for each task. Having a clear schedule ensures that clip updates are not overlooked.

- Monthly Reviews: Conduct monthly reviews of high-use clips to ensure they are current.

- Quarterly Reviews: Review less frequently used clips on a quarterly basis.

- Annual Overhaul: Perform a comprehensive review of the entire clip library annually to identify outdated content and make necessary updates.

9. Use Tags and Metadata

Tags and metadata can help you organize and update your clips more efficiently. By assigning relevant tags and metadata to each clip, you can quickly locate clips that need updates and track changes over time.

- Tagging: Use descriptive tags to categorize clips by topic, department, or project. This makes it easier to find and update related clips.

- Metadata Fields: Add metadata fields such as "Last Updated Date" and "Updated By" to each clip. This information helps you track when a clip was last reviewed and updated.

10. Encourage a Culture of Continuous Improvement

Foster a culture of continuous improvement within your team. Encourage team members to regularly review and update clips and to share best practices for maintaining an up-to-date clip library. Recognize and reward efforts to keep the clip library current and relevant.

- Continuous Feedback: Create an environment where team members feel comfortable providing feedback on clip content and suggesting updates.

- Recognition and Rewards: Recognize and reward team members who contribute to keeping the clip library up-to-date. This can be done through formal recognition programs or informal praise.

Conclusion

Keeping your ClipCharm clips up-to-date is essential for maintaining a valuable and effective clip library. By scheduling regular reviews, implementing version control, leveraging ClipCharm's features, collaborating with your team, and fostering a culture of continuous improvement, you can ensure that your clips remain current and useful. An up-to-date clip library not only improves productivity but also enhances collaboration and ensures that your team has access to the most accurate and relevant information.

CHAPTER VI
Troubleshooting and Support

6.1 Common Issues and Solutions

When working with ClipCharm in Microsoft 365, users might encounter a variety of issues. Understanding these common problems and knowing how to solve them is crucial for maintaining a smooth workflow. This chapter will help you troubleshoot and resolve some of the most frequent issues users face.

6.1.1 Installation Problems

Installation problems can be a significant hindrance when first setting up ClipCharm. These issues can stem from various sources, including compatibility issues, missing prerequisites, network restrictions, or user permissions. Below are some common installation problems and their solutions.

1. Compatibility Issues

One of the first things to check if you encounter installation problems is the compatibility of ClipCharm with your operating system and Microsoft 365 version.

Solution:

- Check System Requirements: Ensure that your system meets the minimum requirements for ClipCharm. These typically include a specific version of the operating system (e.g., Windows 10) and Microsoft 365.

- Update Software: Make sure both your operating system and Microsoft 365 are up-to-date. Install the latest updates and patches to avoid compatibility issues.

- Download the Correct Version: Verify that you have downloaded the correct version of ClipCharm that corresponds to your operating system and Microsoft 365 version.

2. Missing Prerequisites

Sometimes, ClipCharm requires additional software components or updates that are not present on your system.

Solution:

- Install Required Software: Check the installation documentation for any additional software requirements such as .NET Framework, specific runtime libraries, or service packs.

- Run Windows Update: Use Windows Update to ensure all necessary system updates and components are installed.

3. Network Restrictions

Network-related issues can also prevent successful installation, especially in a corporate environment where firewalls and proxy servers are common.

Solution:

- Check Network Connection: Ensure that your internet connection is stable. A weak or intermittent connection can cause download or installation failures.

- Adjust Firewall Settings: Temporarily disable your firewall or antivirus software to see if they are blocking the installation process. If the installation succeeds, add ClipCharm to the list of allowed programs.

- Configure Proxy Settings: If you are behind a proxy server, configure your proxy settings in the network settings of your system or during the ClipCharm installation process.

4. Insufficient Permissions

Installation issues can also arise from not having the necessary administrative privileges on your system.

Solution:

- Run as Administrator: Right-click the installation file and select "Run as administrator." This grants the installer the necessary permissions to make changes to your system.

- Check User Account: Ensure that you are logged into an account with administrative privileges. Standard user accounts may not have the necessary permissions to install new software.

5. Corrupted Installation Files

Occasionally, the installation files themselves may be corrupted or incomplete.

Solution:

- Re-download the Installer: Download a fresh copy of the installation file from the official ClipCharm website. Sometimes files can become corrupted during the download process.

- Verify File Integrity: If available, use checksums or other verification methods to ensure the integrity of the downloaded file.

6. Conflicting Software

Existing software on your system might conflict with the installation process.

Solution:

- Close Running Applications: Close all other applications before starting the installation to prevent conflicts.

- Uninstall Conflicting Software: If you identify a specific software causing the conflict, consider uninstalling it temporarily until ClipCharm is successfully installed.

- Check for Known Conflicts: Refer to the ClipCharm support documentation for any known software conflicts and follow the recommended steps to resolve them.

Step-by-Step Troubleshooting Guide

To provide a more structured approach, here is a step-by-step troubleshooting guide to resolve installation problems with ClipCharm:

1. Verify System Compatibility:

   - Check the official ClipCharm system requirements.

   - Ensure your operating system and Microsoft 365 are up-to-date.

2. Check Prerequisites:

   - Install any required software components.

   - Run Windows Update to ensure all necessary updates are installed.

3. Resolve Network Issues:

   - Confirm a stable internet connection.

   - Adjust firewall or antivirus settings if necessary.

   - Configure proxy settings as needed.

4. Ensure Sufficient Permissions:

   - Run the installer as an administrator.

   - Confirm you are using an account with administrative privileges.

5. Address Installation File Issues:

   - Re-download the installation file from the official source.

   - Verify the integrity of the downloaded file.

6. Identify and Mitigate Software Conflicts:

   - Close all other running applications.

   - Uninstall any conflicting software temporarily.

   - Refer to ClipCharm documentation for known conflicts.

Case Studies Here are a few real-world case studies that illustrate how users resolved their installation problems:

Case Study 1: Compatibility Issues

- Problem: John was unable to install ClipCharm on his Windows 7 machine.

- Solution: Upon checking the system requirements, John realized that ClipCharm required Windows 10. After upgrading his operating system, the installation proceeded without any issues.

Case Study 2: Network Restrictions

- Problem: Maria experienced download errors during the installation of ClipCharm due to her corporate network's firewall.

- Solution: Maria temporarily disabled her firewall and antivirus software, then successfully installed ClipCharm. She later added ClipCharm to the list of allowed programs in her firewall settings to avoid future issues.

Case Study 3: Insufficient Permissions

- Problem: Alex encountered an error message stating he did not have sufficient permissions to install ClipCharm.

- Solution: By right-clicking the installation file and selecting "Run as administrator," Alex was able to complete the installation process without further issues.

Conclusion

Installation problems with ClipCharm can be frustrating, but they are typically solvable with the right approach. By systematically checking compatibility, prerequisites, network settings, permissions, file integrity, and potential software conflicts, you can overcome most installation hurdles. Refer to the step-by-step troubleshooting guide and case studies provided in this section to resolve common installation issues and ensure a smooth start with ClipCharm in Microsoft 365.

6.1.2 ClipCharm Performance Issues

ClipCharm is designed to enhance productivity by providing robust features for managing and sharing clips within the Microsoft 365 ecosystem. However, like any software, users may encounter performance issues that can affect its efficiency and usability. This section will address common performance problems users might face with ClipCharm and provide practical solutions to resolve them.

Common Performance Issues

1. Slow Clip Loading

Issue Description: Users may notice that clips take longer to load than usual, which can hinder workflow efficiency. This delay might manifest as slow response times when opening or editing clips.

Potential Causes:

- Large Clip Size: Clips with large amounts of data or high-resolution content can take longer to load.

- Network Connectivity: Poor or unstable network connections can affect the loading speed of clips, especially when they are stored in the cloud.

- System Performance: Low system resources, such as RAM and CPU, can slow down the performance of ClipCharm.

Solutions:

- Optimize Clip Size: Reduce the size of clips by compressing images or removing unnecessary data. Use ClipCharm's built-in tools for resizing or editing clips to manage their size effectively.

- Improve Network Connectivity: Ensure that your internet connection is stable and has sufficient bandwidth. Consider using a wired connection if possible, or connect to a higher-speed network.

- Upgrade System Resources: Check your system's performance and consider upgrading hardware components if necessary. Increasing RAM or upgrading the processor can help improve overall performance.

2. Lag During Editing

Issue Description: Users may experience lag or delays when editing clips, which can disrupt the workflow and affect productivity.

Potential Causes:

- Heavy Editing Operations: Performing complex edits or applying multiple changes to a clip can cause performance lag.

- Background Processes: Other applications or processes running on your system can consume resources, leading to decreased performance in ClipCharm.

Solutions:

- Simplify Edits: Break down complex editing tasks into smaller, manageable steps. Apply edits gradually to reduce the processing load.

- Close Unnecessary Applications: Shut down or minimize other applications and processes running on your system to free up resources for ClipCharm.

3. ClipCharm Crashes or Freezes

Issue Description: In some cases, ClipCharm may crash or freeze unexpectedly, causing users to lose progress and experience interruptions.

Potential Causes:

- Software Bugs: Bugs or glitches within ClipCharm can lead to crashes or freezes.

- Conflicts with Other Software: Incompatibilities with other installed software or add-ins can cause stability issues.

- Corrupted Files: Corrupted clip files or settings may trigger application crashes.

Solutions:

- Update ClipCharm: Ensure that you are using the latest version of ClipCharm. Updates often include bug fixes and performance improvements. Check for updates regularly and install them promptly.

- Check for Software Conflicts: Disable or uninstall conflicting software or add-ins that may be affecting ClipCharm. Perform a clean boot to identify potential conflicts.

- Repair or Reinstall ClipCharm: If crashes persist, consider repairing or reinstalling ClipCharm. This process can resolve issues caused by corrupted files or settings.

4. Slow Syncing with Microsoft 365

Issue Description: Users may experience slow synchronization between ClipCharm and other Microsoft 365 applications, which can affect data consistency and accessibility.

Potential Causes:

- Syncing Conflicts: Conflicts between local and cloud versions of clips can cause synchronization delays.

- Large Data Volumes: Syncing large volumes of data or numerous clips can slow down the process.

Solutions:

- Resolve Sync Conflicts: Check for and resolve any conflicts between local and cloud versions of clips. Ensure that changes are consistent across all devices.

- Manage Data Volumes: Regularly archive or delete unnecessary clips to reduce the volume of data being synced. This can help improve synchronization speed.

5. Search Function Lag

Issue Description: Users may experience delays when using the search function to locate clips, impacting their ability to find and access information quickly.

Potential Causes:

- Indexing Issues: Problems with indexing can affect search performance and accuracy.

- Large Clip Library: A large number of clips can slow down search operations.

Solutions:

- Rebuild Index: Rebuild the search index to improve search performance. Follow ClipCharm's instructions for indexing and optimizing search.

- Organize Clip Library: Regularly organize and categorize clips to streamline the search process. Implement a consistent naming convention and tagging system to enhance search efficiency.

Preventive Measures

To minimize the risk of performance issues with ClipCharm, consider implementing the following preventive measures:

1. Regular Maintenance:

   - Perform regular maintenance tasks, such as clearing cache and temporary files, to keep ClipCharm running smoothly.

   - Update ClipCharm and Microsoft 365 regularly to benefit from the latest improvements and security fixes.

2. System Optimization:

   - Ensure that your system meets the recommended hardware and software requirements for ClipCharm. Regularly check for and address system performance issues.

   - Use system optimization tools to enhance overall performance and free up resources for ClipCharm.

3. Data Management:

   - Implement effective data management practices, such as archiving old clips and organizing your clip library. This helps prevent data overload and improves performance.

Conclusion

Addressing performance issues with ClipCharm requires a combination of troubleshooting techniques and preventive measures. By understanding common performance problems and implementing practical solutions, users can maintain optimal performance and enhance their productivity with ClipCharm in Microsoft 365. Regular maintenance, system optimization, and effective data management are key to ensuring a smooth and efficient experience with ClipCharm.

6.2 Accessing Help and Support

6.2.1 Using ClipCharm Help Resources

Introduction

ClipCharm is designed to enhance productivity and streamline content management within Microsoft 365. To fully utilize its features and troubleshoot any issues, users need access to comprehensive help resources. This section will guide you through the various help resources available for ClipCharm, including how to use them effectively.

1. In-Application Help

ClipCharm provides an integrated help system accessible directly within the application. This feature is designed to offer contextual assistance as you work, ensuring you can find relevant information without leaving the application.

1.1 Accessing In-Application Help

To access the in-application help:

1. Open ClipCharm: Launch the ClipCharm application from your Microsoft 365 suite.

2. Locate the Help Icon: Usually represented by a question mark icon or labeled "Help" in the application's toolbar or menu.

3. Click the Help Icon: This will open a help panel or window within the application.

1.2 Features of In-Application Help

- Contextual Help: Provides information based on the current task or screen you are viewing.

- Search Functionality: Allows you to search for specific topics or keywords related to your query.

- How-To Guides: Includes step-by-step instructions for common tasks.

- Troubleshooting Tips: Offers solutions to common issues you may encounter.

1.3 Navigating In-Application Help

- Search Bar: Use the search bar to enter keywords or phrases related to your issue.

- Help Topics: Browse through categorized help topics to find relevant information.

- FAQs: Frequently Asked Questions section provides quick answers to common problems.

2. Online Documentation

ClipCharm's online documentation offers a comprehensive repository of guides, tutorials, and reference materials. This resource is ideal for users who need detailed information or want to explore advanced features.

2.1 Accessing Online Documentation

To access the online documentation:

1. Visit the ClipCharm Website: Go to the official ClipCharm website or the specific support page dedicated to ClipCharm.

2. Navigate to the Documentation Section: Look for links to "Documentation," "Support," or "Resources."

3. Select the Desired Document: Choose from user manuals, quick start guides, or detailed technical documentation.

2.2 Features of Online Documentation

- User Manuals: Comprehensive guides covering all aspects of ClipCharm.

- Quick Start Guides: Short guides for new users to get started quickly.

- Technical References: Detailed information on advanced features and configurations.

- Video Tutorials: Step-by-step video guides demonstrating various functions.

2.3 Searching in Online Documentation

- Search Functionality: Use the search bar to find specific topics or keywords.

- Table of Contents: Navigate through the table of contents to locate relevant sections.

- Index: Use the index to find topics by keyword or subject.

3. ClipCharm Support Community

The ClipCharm support community provides a platform for users to ask questions, share experiences, and get advice from other users and experts.

3.1 Accessing the Support Community

To access the ClipCharm support community:

1. Visit the Community Forum: Navigate to the official ClipCharm community forum or discussion board.

2. Create an Account: If required, create an account or log in to participate.

3. Browse or Search: Browse through existing threads or use the search function to find discussions related to your issue.

3.2 Features of the Support Community

- Forums: Participate in discussions about various ClipCharm topics.

- Q&A Sections: Ask questions and get answers from other users or community experts.

- Knowledge Base: Access a collection of articles and posts about common issues and solutions.

- User Contributions: Benefit from the experiences and solutions shared by other users.

3.3 Engaging with the Community

- Posting Questions: Write detailed descriptions of your issues or questions to get accurate responses.

- Providing Answers: Contribute solutions and advice based on your own experiences.

- Following Topics: Stay updated on discussions and new solutions related to ClipCharm.

4. Contacting ClipCharm Support

When in-app help, online documentation, and the support community do not resolve your issue, contacting ClipCharm's customer support may be necessary.

4.1 Contact Methods

- Email Support: Send an email to the support team with detailed information about your issue.

- Phone Support: Call the support hotline for direct assistance.

- Live Chat: Use the live chat feature on the ClipCharm website for real-time help.

- Support Ticket System: Submit a support ticket through the website or application for tracking and resolution.

4.2 Providing Effective Information

When contacting support:

- Include Detailed Information: Provide a thorough description of the issue, including error messages and screenshots if possible.

- Specify Your Environment: Include details about your ClipCharm version, operating system, and any other relevant software.

- Follow Up: Keep track of your support request and follow up if necessary.

4.3 Expected Response Times

- Email Support: Typically receives a response within 24-48 hours.

- Phone Support: Immediate assistance during business hours.

- Live Chat: Real-time support during available hours.

- Support Ticket System: Response times may vary depending on the complexity of the issue.

5. Additional Resources

In addition to the primary help resources, various supplementary materials can aid in resolving issues and learning more about ClipCharm.

5.1 Third-Party Tutorials and Reviews

- YouTube Tutorials: Search for video tutorials on YouTube for visual step-by-step guides.

- Tech Blogs: Read reviews and tutorials from technology bloggers and industry experts.

5.2 Training and Certification

- Online Courses: Enroll in online courses to deepen your understanding of ClipCharm.

- Certification Programs: Obtain certification to validate your expertise in using ClipCharm.

Conclusion

Using the help resources available for ClipCharm is crucial for resolving issues and maximizing the benefits of the application. By utilizing in-application help, online documentation, the support community, and direct support channels, users can effectively address problems and enhance their productivity. For ongoing support, staying engaged with community resources and exploring additional learning opportunities will further ensure a smooth and efficient experience with ClipCharm in Microsoft 365.

6.2.2 Contacting Support

In the realm of digital tools and software, encountering issues is almost inevitable. Whether you're facing technical glitches, configuration problems, or need guidance on how to use certain features, knowing how to effectively contact support can save you time and frustration. For ClipCharm users within the Microsoft 365 ecosystem, accessing support is a crucial aspect of ensuring smooth and efficient use of the software. This section will guide you through various methods for contacting support, including how to make the most of each option, what information to provide, and how to follow up effectively.

Understanding the Support Structure

Before diving into the methods for contacting support, it's essential to understand the support structure provided by ClipCharm and Microsoft 365. Support services are generally structured into several tiers, each designed to address different levels of issues:

1. Self-Service Support: Basic troubleshooting and assistance are often available through self-service resources, including knowledge bases, FAQs, and user forums.

2. Community Support: This involves leveraging user communities and forums where you can seek help from other users and experts who might have faced similar issues.

3. Direct Support: For more complex or unresolved issues, direct support channels such as email, phone, or live chat with support representatives are available.

Methods for Contacting Support

1. Microsoft 365 Support Portal

The Microsoft 365 Support Portal is the primary channel for accessing official support for ClipCharm and other Microsoft 365 services. Here's how to navigate and use it effectively:

- Accessing the Portal: Go to the [Microsoft 365 Support Portal](https://support.microsoft.com/). You may need to sign in with your Microsoft 365 account to access certain features.

- Navigating the Portal: Use the search bar to find articles related to your issue. If you can't find a solution, you can submit a support request. The portal provides various options including submitting a ticket, requesting a call, or starting a live chat.

- Submitting a Support Request: When submitting a support request, provide a detailed description of the issue, including any error messages, screenshots, and steps to reproduce the problem. The more information you provide, the quicker and more accurately the support team can address your issue.

- Tracking Your Request: After submitting a request, you'll receive a confirmation email with a reference number. You can use this number to track the status of your request and follow up if needed.

2. ClipCharm Support Resources

ClipCharm offers dedicated support resources that are specifically tailored to issues related to its application:

- ClipCharm Help Center: Access https://clipchamp.com/en/ for detailed articles, guides, and troubleshooting tips. This resource is ideal for finding solutions to common problems and learning more about ClipCharm's features.

- In-App Support: Many software applications, including ClipCharm, offer in-app support options. Look for a "Help" or "Support" button within the application, which can provide direct links to support resources or initiate a support request.

- Email Support: If the Help Center and in-app options do not resolve your issue, you can contact ClipCharm's support team via email. Send a detailed email to support@clipcharm.com with information about your issue, including any relevant screenshots and steps to reproduce the problem. Response times may vary, so be sure to monitor your email for updates.

3. Live Chat and Phone Support

For urgent issues or real-time assistance, live chat and phone support are effective methods:

- Live Chat: The Microsoft 365 Support Portal often offers a live chat option where you can interact with a support representative in real time. This can be particularly useful for getting quick answers to specific questions or resolving minor issues.

- Phone Support: If you prefer speaking directly to a support representative, phone support is available. Contact Microsoft 365 support at the designated phone number for your region, which can be found on the [Microsoft Support Contact Page](https://support.microsoft.com/contactus). Be prepared to provide your account information and a description of your issue.

4. Social Media and Online Forums

In addition to official support channels, social media and online forums can be valuable resources:

- Social Media: Follow ClipCharm and Microsoft 365 on platforms like Twitter, LinkedIn, and Facebook for updates, tips, and direct support interactions. Many companies have dedicated social media teams that can address questions and escalate issues.

- Online Forums: Participate in online forums such as Reddit or specialized tech forums where users discuss ClipCharm and Microsoft 365. These forums can be helpful for finding community-driven solutions and tips.

Providing Effective Support Requests

When contacting support, the quality of your request can significantly impact the efficiency and effectiveness of the resolution. Here's how to ensure your support request is as effective as possible:

1. Be Specific: Clearly describe the issue you're facing. Include relevant details such as error messages, the steps you've taken, and the specific feature or function that is problematic.

2. Provide Context: Include information about your environment, such as the version of ClipCharm you're using, your operating system, and any recent changes to your setup.

3. Attach Evidence: Provide screenshots, error logs, or other evidence that can help support staff understand and diagnose the problem more quickly.

4. Follow Up: If you don't receive a response within the expected timeframe, follow up with the support team using your reference number. Persistence can help ensure your issue is addressed promptly.

Tracking and Managing Your Support Requests

Once you've submitted a support request, managing and tracking it effectively is key to resolving your issue:

- Monitor Your Email: Check your email regularly for updates on your support request. Be responsive to any requests for additional information from the support team.

- Use the Support Portal: If you submitted a request through the Microsoft 365 Support Portal or ClipCharm's support site, use the portal to check the status of your request and view any updates or responses.

- Document the Process: Keep a record of all communications and steps taken during the support process. This can be useful for future reference or if you need to escalate the issue.

Conclusion

Effective support is crucial for overcoming challenges and maximizing the benefits of ClipCharm in Microsoft 365. By understanding the available support options and following best practices for contacting and managing support requests, you can ensure that you receive timely and accurate assistance. Whether through self-service resources, direct support channels, or community forums, the right support can make a significant difference in resolving issues and enhancing your overall experience with ClipCharm.

6.3 Community Resources and Learning Opportunities

6.3.1 ClipCharm User Community

The ClipCharm User Community is an invaluable resource for both new and experienced users of the ClipCharm tool within Microsoft 365. This section delves into the various aspects of the ClipCharm User Community, explaining how it can enhance your experience with ClipCharm and how to effectively utilize this resource to address issues, learn new techniques, and stay informed about the latest updates.

Overview of the ClipCharm User Community

The ClipCharm User Community is a collective of users, ranging from beginners to advanced professionals, who come together to share knowledge, offer support, and discuss various aspects of ClipCharm. This community operates through various platforms, including official forums, social media groups, and dedicated websites. Engaging with this community can provide numerous benefits, such as access to a wealth of collective knowledge, solutions to common problems, and opportunities for networking.

Platforms and Forums

1. Official ClipCharm Forums: The official forums are often the central hub for discussions related to ClipCharm. These forums are usually moderated by ClipCharm support teams and experienced users, ensuring that the information shared is accurate and reliable. Users can post questions, share solutions, and engage in discussions about various ClipCharm features and issues.

   - Benefits: Access to structured threads, direct interaction with ClipCharm staff, and organized categories for different topics.

   - How to Access: Typically accessible through the ClipCharm website or Microsoft 365 support portal.

2. Social Media Groups: Social media platforms such as LinkedIn, Facebook, and Twitter often host groups and pages dedicated to ClipCharm users. These groups provide a more informal setting for users to interact, share tips, and discuss their experiences with ClipCharm.

- Benefits: Real-time updates, informal discussions, and networking opportunities with other users.

- How to Join: Search for ClipCharm-related groups on social media platforms and request to join.

3. Dedicated Websites and Blogs: Various websites and blogs are dedicated to ClipCharm and its usage within Microsoft 365. These sites often feature tutorials, user experiences, and tips from experts.

- Benefits: Access to detailed articles, how-to guides, and expert opinions.

- How to Find: Search for ClipCharm-related blogs and websites through search engines or recommendations from the community.

How to Engage with the Community

1. Participate in Discussions: Engaging in discussions on forums and social media groups allows users to ask questions, share their knowledge, and learn from others. Active participation can help users find solutions to their problems and contribute to the community's growth.

- Tips for Effective Participation: Be clear and concise in your questions and responses, provide context when discussing issues, and be respectful of other users.

2. Share Your Knowledge: Experienced users can contribute by sharing their insights and solutions. Posting detailed responses and creating tutorials or guides can help others who might be facing similar challenges.

- How to Share: Write detailed posts or create video tutorials addressing common issues or advanced techniques, and share them on relevant forums or social media groups.

3. Ask Questions and Seek Help: When facing issues with ClipCharm, asking for help in the community can provide quick solutions and alternative approaches. Be specific about the problem and include relevant details to get accurate responses.

 - How to Ask: Clearly describe the issue, mention any troubleshooting steps you have already taken, and provide any error messages or screenshots if applicable.

4. Stay Updated: Follow community discussions and announcements to stay informed about new features, updates, and best practices. Engaging with the community regularly ensures that you are aware of the latest developments and can make the most of ClipCharm.

 - How to Stay Informed: Subscribe to forums, follow social media groups, and read community blogs to receive updates and announcements.

Benefits of Engaging with the ClipCharm User Community

1. Access to Collective Knowledge: The community comprises users with diverse experiences and expertise. This collective knowledge can provide valuable insights and solutions that may not be available through official documentation.

2. Real-Time Problem Solving: Community members often provide solutions to problems faster than waiting for official support. Engaging with the community can lead to quicker resolutions and workarounds.

3. Networking Opportunities: Connecting with other ClipCharm users can lead to professional networking opportunities, collaborations, and even career advancements. The community provides a platform for making valuable connections.

4. Learning Opportunities: The community is a great place to learn new techniques, discover best practices, and stay updated on industry trends. Engaging with other users can expose you to innovative ways of using ClipCharm.

Common Community Practices

1. Respectful Communication: Maintaining a respectful and courteous tone in discussions is essential for a positive community experience. Respecting diverse opinions and providing constructive feedback fosters a healthy environment.

2. Following Community Guidelines: Most communities have guidelines or rules that users are expected to follow. Adhering to these guidelines ensures that interactions remain professional and focused.

3. Providing Feedback: Sharing feedback about your experiences with ClipCharm can help improve the tool and contribute to the community's growth. Constructive feedback can be valuable for developers and other users.

Conclusion

The ClipCharm User Community is a vital resource for maximizing your experience with ClipCharm in Microsoft 365. By actively engaging with the community, users can gain valuable insights, solve problems more efficiently, and stay informed about the latest developments. Whether you are a new user seeking guidance or an experienced professional looking to share your knowledge, the community offers numerous opportunities for learning and collaboration.

Engage with the community through various platforms, participate in discussions, and make the most of the collective knowledge available. By doing so, you not only enhance your own ClipCharm experience but also contribute to the success and growth of the community as a whole.

6.3.2 Online Courses and Tutorials

In today's digital landscape, continuous learning is essential, particularly when it comes to mastering new tools like ClipCharm in Microsoft 365. Online courses and tutorials are invaluable resources that offer structured learning paths and practical knowledge for both beginners and advanced users. This section delves into various online courses and tutorials available for ClipCharm, providing a comprehensive guide to help users expand their skills and expertise.

1. Importance of Online Learning for ClipCharm

Online courses and tutorials are not only convenient but also highly effective for learning ClipCharm. They provide users with the flexibility to learn at their own pace, revisit complex topics, and access expert guidance from anywhere in the world. For users who are new to ClipCharm or looking to enhance their existing knowledge, these resources can be instrumental in understanding advanced features, solving specific problems, and optimizing their use of the tool.

2. Types of Online Learning Resources

Online learning resources for ClipCharm come in various formats, each catering to different learning preferences and needs. The main types include:

- Video Tutorials: These are visual demonstrations of ClipCharm's features and functionalities. They can range from short, focused videos addressing specific tasks to comprehensive courses that cover the entire tool.

- Interactive Courses: Structured courses that often include quizzes, hands-on exercises, and interactive content. These are designed to provide a thorough understanding of ClipCharm, with assessments to track progress.

- Webinars: Live or recorded sessions led by experts or experienced users. Webinars offer real-time interaction and the opportunity to ask questions.

- Documentation and E-Books: Detailed written guides that provide in-depth explanations of ClipCharm's features, often accompanied by screenshots and step-by-step instructions.

3. Recommended Online Courses

Several reputable platforms offer high-quality online courses for ClipCharm users. Here are some of the top options:

3.1. Microsoft Learn

Microsoft Learn is a platform developed by Microsoft that offers free, self-paced learning paths and modules. For ClipCharm, users can find relevant courses that cover the basics as well as advanced features.

- Course Highlights:

  - Introduction to ClipCharm: Basic functionalities and setup.

  - Advanced Features: Detailed exploration of advanced tools and integrations.

  - Practical Exercises: Hands-on activities to reinforce learning.

Microsoft Learn is an excellent starting point for those new to ClipCharm and Microsoft 365, as it provides a strong foundation in the context of Microsoft's ecosystem.

3.2. Udemy

Udemy offers a variety of courses tailored to different levels of expertise. Courses related to ClipCharm on Udemy often include video lectures, quizzes, and downloadable resources.

- Popular Courses:

  - "ClipCharm Fundamentals for Microsoft 365": A comprehensive course covering basic to intermediate features of ClipCharm.

  - "Mastering ClipCharm: From Beginner to Advanced": An in-depth course focusing on advanced functionalities and best practices.

Udemy's courses are generally designed by industry professionals and often include real-world examples and case studies, making them practical and relevant.

3.3. LinkedIn Learning

LinkedIn Learning provides professional development courses, including those for ClipCharm. The courses are often created by experienced trainers and come with certificates upon completion.

- Course Options:

  - "Getting Started with ClipCharm": An introductory course focusing on the essential features and setup.

- "Advanced ClipCharm Techniques": For users who want to dive deeper into advanced features and integrations.

LinkedIn Learning is ideal for professionals looking to enhance their skills and add credentials to their profiles.

3.4. Coursera

Coursera partners with universities and organizations to offer high-quality courses, including those for software tools like ClipCharm.

- Highlighted Courses:

  - "ClipCharm and Microsoft 365 Integration": Focuses on how ClipCharm integrates with other Microsoft 365 tools.

  - "Effective Use of ClipCharm for Business": Practical applications and case studies for businesses.

Coursera's courses are often more academic in nature and provide a thorough understanding of both theoretical and practical aspects of ClipCharm.

4. How to Choose the Right Course

Selecting the right online course for ClipCharm depends on several factors:

- Skill Level: Beginners should start with introductory courses, while advanced users might look for more specialized content.

- Learning Style: Consider whether you prefer video lectures, interactive content, or written materials.

- Course Reviews and Ratings: Check user feedback to ensure the course meets your expectations and offers valuable content.

- Cost: While many courses are free, some premium options may require payment. Assess your budget and the value offered by each course.

5. How to Maximize Learning from Online Courses

To get the most out of online courses and tutorials for ClipCharm, consider the following tips:

- Set Clear Goals: Define what you want to achieve from the course. This will help you stay focused and motivated.

- Practice Regularly: Apply what you learn by working on real projects or exercises. Hands-on practice is crucial for mastering ClipCharm.

- Engage with the Community: Participate in course forums or discussion groups to interact with other learners and instructors.

- Take Notes: Document key points and techniques learned during the course for future reference.

- Seek Feedback: If available, seek feedback on your progress from instructors or peers.

6. Additional Learning Resources

In addition to structured courses, there are other resources that can complement your learning:

- YouTube Channels: Many experts and enthusiasts create tutorials and walkthroughs on YouTube. Channels like Microsoft Office Tutorials or TechSmith Tutorials often cover ClipCharm and related tools.

- Blogs and Articles: Industry blogs and websites sometimes publish in-depth articles and how-tos. Look for posts on Microsoft's official blog or tech websites like TechCrunch.

- Online Forums: Engage with online communities such as Reddit or Stack Exchange to ask questions, share knowledge, and learn from others' experiences.

7. Keeping Up-to-Date with ClipCharm

The landscape of software tools is constantly evolving. To stay current with ClipCharm:

- Follow Updates: Regularly check for updates from Microsoft regarding new features or changes in ClipCharm.

- Subscribe to Newsletters: Sign up for newsletters from Microsoft or relevant tech blogs.

- Attend Webinars and Workshops: Participate in live sessions and workshops to gain insights into the latest developments and best practices.

8. Conclusion

Online courses and tutorials are essential resources for mastering ClipCharm in Microsoft 365. By leveraging these resources, users can enhance their skills, stay updated with the latest features, and ultimately improve their productivity and efficiency. Whether you are a beginner or an advanced user, there is a wealth of information available online to help you make the most of ClipCharm.

As you explore these learning opportunities, remember to stay engaged, practice regularly, and apply your knowledge to real-world scenarios. With the right approach, you'll be well-equipped to harness the full potential of ClipCharm and integrate it effectively into your Microsoft 365 workflow.

CHAPTER VII
Future Trends and Developments

7.1 The Future of ClipCharm

7.1.1 Upcoming Features and Updates

As technology continues to evolve, so too does ClipCharm within the Microsoft 365 ecosystem. With an ever-expanding user base and increasing demands for enhanced functionalities, ClipCharm's development team is dedicated to continually improving the platform. This section explores the upcoming features and updates that are set to enhance the user experience and expand the capabilities of ClipCharm in Microsoft 365.

Enhanced Integration with Microsoft 365 Applications

One of the primary focuses for ClipCharm's future updates is to deepen its integration with other Microsoft 365 applications. As businesses increasingly rely on a suite of tools to manage their operations, seamless integration becomes crucial. Upcoming updates will aim to provide enhanced connectivity with:

- Microsoft Teams: The integration with Microsoft Teams is expected to become more robust, allowing users to directly share and manage clips within team channels and chats. This integration will also enable real-time collaborative editing and discussion of clips, making teamwork more efficient.

- SharePoint: Upcoming updates will enhance the integration with SharePoint, allowing users to easily link and manage clips stored in SharePoint libraries. Improved synchronization will facilitate smoother access to clips within SharePoint sites and enable more dynamic content management.

- OneDrive: Improved integration with OneDrive will provide users with enhanced options for storing and accessing clips. Expect updates to streamline the process of saving clips to OneDrive, ensuring that files are automatically backed up and accessible across devices.

Advanced Clip Management Features

To address the needs of users managing extensive clip libraries, future updates will introduce advanced clip management features:

- Smart Tagging and Categorization: ClipCharm will soon offer advanced tagging and categorization capabilities. Users will be able to apply smart tags based on clip content, usage patterns, and metadata. This feature will facilitate better organization and retrieval of clips.

- Enhanced Search Functionality: The search functionality will be significantly improved to support more granular search queries. Users will be able to search for clips using keywords, tags, and even visual content recognition. This will make finding specific clips quicker and more intuitive.

- Automated Organization: Upcoming features will include automated organization tools that use machine learning to categorize and sort clips based on user behavior and content type. This will reduce the time spent manually organizing clips and improve overall efficiency.

Improved User Interface and Experience

User experience is a key focus for ClipCharm's future updates. The platform will see several enhancements aimed at making it more user-friendly and visually appealing:

- Redesigned Dashboard: The user interface will receive a comprehensive redesign to provide a more intuitive and streamlined experience. The new dashboard will offer customizable widgets and a more organized layout, allowing users to easily access their most-used features and clips.

- Enhanced Customization Options: Users will gain more control over how they customize their ClipCharm workspace. New options will allow for personalized layouts, color schemes, and theme settings to match individual preferences and improve usability.

- Interactive Tutorials and Guides: To assist new users and those exploring new features, interactive tutorials and guides will be integrated into the platform. These will offer step-by-step instructions and tips on using advanced features, making the learning curve less steep.

Advanced Analytics and Reporting

As businesses increasingly rely on data-driven decisions, ClipCharm will introduce advanced analytics and reporting features:

- Usage Analytics: Future updates will include detailed usage analytics, allowing users to track how frequently clips are accessed, shared, and edited. This data will provide insights into user behavior and content popularity, helping to inform strategic decisions.

- Custom Reports: Users will be able to generate custom reports based on various metrics, such as clip engagement, collaboration frequency, and storage usage. These reports will be exportable in various formats, making it easier to share insights with stakeholders.

Enhanced Security and Compliance Features

With growing concerns around data security and compliance, ClipCharm will bolster its security features to ensure user data is protected:

- Advanced Encryption: Future updates will enhance data encryption both at rest and in transit. This will ensure that all clips and associated data are secure from unauthorized access and potential breaches.

- Compliance Tools: ClipCharm will integrate additional compliance tools to help users meet industry-specific regulations and standards. Features such as audit trails, user access controls, and data retention policies will support compliance efforts.

- Security Notifications: Users will receive real-time notifications regarding security events and potential threats. These notifications will help users stay informed about any unusual activities or breaches related to their clip data.

Expansion of ClipCharm's Ecosystem

To support a broader range of use cases, ClipCharm will expand its ecosystem with:

- Third-Party Integrations: Future updates will include integrations with popular third-party applications and services, providing users with more options for extending ClipCharm's functionality. This may include integration with project management tools, CRM systems, and other productivity applications.

- Developer API: A new developer API will be introduced, allowing organizations to build custom integrations and extensions for ClipCharm. This will enable businesses to tailor the platform to their specific needs and workflows.

- Marketplace for Add-Ons: An add-on marketplace will be launched, featuring third-party extensions and enhancements for ClipCharm. Users will be able to explore and install additional features that align with their requirements.

User Feedback and Community Involvement

ClipCharm's development team values user feedback and will continue to engage with the user community to drive future improvements:

- Feedback Mechanisms: Users will have enhanced opportunities to provide feedback through integrated feedback forms and community forums. This will ensure that user suggestions and concerns are considered in the development process.

- Beta Testing Programs: The introduction of beta testing programs will allow users to try out new features before they are officially released. This will provide valuable insights and help refine features based on real-world usage.

- Community Collaboration: The development team will collaborate with the user community through webinars, workshops, and focus groups to gather input and share updates. This collaborative approach will help shape the future direction of ClipCharm.

Conclusion

The future of ClipCharm promises exciting advancements that will enhance its functionality, integration, and user experience within Microsoft 365. From deeper integrations with Microsoft 365 applications to advanced clip management and security features, these upcoming updates aim to empower users and improve productivity. As ClipCharm evolves, staying informed about these developments will help users leverage the platform's full potential and stay ahead in an ever-changing digital landscape.

7.1.2 Industry Trends

As technology evolves at a rapid pace, staying abreast of industry trends is crucial for understanding how tools like ClipCharm will adapt and improve. This section delves into the key industry trends that are likely to influence the future of ClipCharm and similar productivity tools within Microsoft 365. These trends include advancements in artificial intelligence (AI) and machine learning, integration with other technologies, shifts in workplace dynamics, and the increasing focus on user experience and security.

Artificial Intelligence and Machine Learning Integration

1. AI-Powered Features

Artificial Intelligence (AI) and machine learning are transforming various sectors, including productivity tools. For ClipCharm, integrating AI can lead to significant advancements in how users interact with and utilize the tool. AI-powered features could include:

- Smart Recommendations: AI algorithms can analyze user behavior and suggest relevant clips or templates based on past usage patterns. This personalized approach helps users quickly find and use content that is most relevant to their needs.

- Automated Tagging and Categorization: Machine learning algorithms can automatically tag and categorize clips, reducing the manual effort required to organize content. This feature enhances searchability and retrieval efficiency.

- Content Generation: AI can assist in generating content for clips based on user input, such as drafting text or creating basic design elements, thereby streamlining the content creation process.

2. Enhanced Data Insights

AI can also provide deeper insights into user engagement with clips. By analyzing usage patterns, AI can offer actionable insights, such as identifying which clips are most frequently used, how they contribute to productivity, and areas for improvement. These insights can help users optimize their workflow and make data-driven decisions.

Integration with Emerging Technologies

1. Integration with Augmented Reality (AR) and Virtual Reality (VR)

The integration of ClipCharm with Augmented Reality (AR) and Virtual Reality (VR) technologies represents a significant advancement. AR and VR can create immersive experiences for users, enhancing how they interact with clips. For instance:

- AR Enhancements: Users might be able to overlay digital clips onto their physical environment, making it easier to visualize and interact with content in real-world settings.

- VR Collaboration: In a VR environment, users can collaborate on clip creation and editing in a virtual workspace, providing a more interactive and engaging experience.

2. Seamless Integration with Other Microsoft 365 Tools

As Microsoft 365 continues to evolve, ClipCharm will likely benefit from deeper integration with other Microsoft tools. This could include:

- Enhanced Integration with Microsoft Teams: Users might be able to directly insert and collaborate on clips within Teams channels, facilitating real-time collaboration and communication.

- Integration with Microsoft Power Platform: ClipCharm could leverage Microsoft Power Automate and Power Apps to create custom workflows and automate tasks related to clip management.

Shifts in Workplace Dynamics

1. Remote and Hybrid Work Models

The rise of remote and hybrid work models has changed how organizations operate. ClipCharm's future developments will need to address the needs of a distributed workforce:

- Cloud-Based Collaboration: Ensuring that ClipCharm supports seamless cloud-based collaboration is essential for users working from different locations. Features like real-time co-editing and sharing will be crucial.

- Remote Access and Security: As remote work becomes more prevalent, securing clip content and ensuring remote access without compromising data security will be a priority.

2. Emphasis on Collaboration and Communication

In the modern workplace, collaboration and communication tools are critical. ClipCharm will need to focus on enhancing these aspects:

- Integrated Communication Channels: Features that allow users to communicate directly within the tool, such as chat or comment functionalities, can improve collaboration.

- Team-Based Clip Management: Tools that facilitate team-based management of clips, including permissions and version control, will support more effective collaboration.

Focus on User Experience and Accessibility

1. Enhanced User Interface and Experience

The user experience (UX) is central to the success of any productivity tool. Future developments in ClipCharm will likely emphasize:

- Intuitive Design: Continued improvements to the user interface (UI) will make the tool more intuitive and easy to navigate, enhancing overall usability.

- Customization Options: Providing users with more customization options, such as customizable dashboards and themes, will allow them to tailor the tool to their preferences and workflow.

2. Accessibility Features

Ensuring that ClipCharm is accessible to all users, including those with disabilities, is increasingly important. Future updates might include:

- Accessibility Enhancements: Features such as screen reader support, keyboard navigation, and customizable text sizes will make ClipCharm more inclusive.

- Compliance with Accessibility Standards: Adhering to accessibility standards, such as the Web Content Accessibility Guidelines (WCAG), will ensure that the tool is usable by a broader audience.

Security and Privacy Considerations

1. Strengthening Data Security

As data security remains a top priority, ClipCharm will need to continuously enhance its security features:

- Advanced Encryption: Implementing advanced encryption methods to protect clip content from unauthorized access.

- Compliance with Data Protection Regulations: Ensuring compliance with regulations such as GDPR and CCPA to protect user data and privacy.

2. User-Controlled Privacy Settings

Providing users with more control over their privacy settings will be important:

- Granular Permissions: Allowing users to set granular permissions for accessing and sharing clips.

- Transparency in Data Usage: Offering transparency regarding how user data is collected and used by ClipCharm.

Conclusion

As ClipCharm evolves, staying aligned with industry trends will be crucial for its success and relevance. By integrating AI and machine learning, embracing emerging technologies, adapting to shifting workplace dynamics, focusing on user experience and accessibility, and prioritizing security and privacy, ClipCharm will continue to enhance its functionality and support users in their productivity journey within Microsoft 365. Keeping an eye on these trends will ensure that ClipCharm remains a powerful and indispensable tool for users in the ever-changing landscape of modern work.

7.2 Staying Informed About ClipCharm

Keeping abreast of the latest news and announcements regarding ClipCharm is crucial for leveraging its full potential and staying ahead in the ever-evolving landscape of productivity tools. This section will explore various methods and resources you can use to stay updated with the latest developments in ClipCharm.

7.2.1 News and Announcements

Staying informed about the latest news and announcements concerning ClipCharm ensures that users are aware of new features, updates, and other critical information that can enhance their productivity and usage of the tool. Here are several strategies and resources to help you stay up-to-date:

Official ClipCharm Blog

One of the most reliable sources of information about ClipCharm is its official blog. The blog often features detailed posts about new updates, upcoming features, and best practices. Subscribing to the blog or setting up an RSS feed can ensure that you receive the latest information directly in your inbox.

- Why Follow the Blog?

 - Timely Updates: The official blog provides timely updates on new releases, feature enhancements, and important announcements.

 - In-depth Articles: The blog often includes in-depth articles that explain how to use new features and make the most out of existing ones.

 - Expert Insights: Articles are usually written by experts who provide insights and tips that can be very useful for users at all levels.

Email Newsletters

Subscribing to ClipCharm's email newsletters is another excellent way to stay informed. These newsletters typically contain a roundup of the most important updates, tips, and announcements.

- *Benefits of Newsletters:*

  - Convenience: Newsletters deliver the latest news directly to your email, making it easy to stay informed without having to actively seek out information.

  - Curated Content: Newsletters often curate the most relevant and important content, saving you time.

  - Exclusive Information: Sometimes, newsletters provide exclusive insights or early access to new features.

Social Media Channels

ClipCharm maintains an active presence on various social media platforms. Following their official accounts on Twitter, LinkedIn, Facebook, and other platforms can keep you in the loop about the latest announcements and updates.

- Advantages of Social Media:

  - Real-time Updates: Social media platforms provide real-time updates, ensuring that you are among the first to know about any new developments.

  - Engagement: Social media allows for direct engagement with the ClipCharm team and other users, facilitating discussions and feedback.

  - Diverse Content: Social media channels often share a variety of content, including videos, infographics, and user stories.

Webinars and Online Events

ClipCharm frequently hosts webinars and online events to showcase new features, provide training, and discuss best practices. Attending these events can offer valuable insights and a deeper understanding of the tool's capabilities.

- Why Attend Webinars?

- Live Demonstrations: Webinars often include live demonstrations of new features, giving you a firsthand look at how they work.

- Interactive Q&A: Most webinars have a Q&A session where you can ask questions and get answers from experts.

- Networking: Webinars provide an opportunity to connect with other users and share experiences.

Community Forums

Participating in ClipCharm's community forums is another effective way to stay informed. These forums are a hub for user-generated content, discussions, and shared knowledge.

- *Benefits of Community Forums:*

- Peer Support: Forums allow you to connect with other users who might have similar questions or experiences.

- Crowdsourced Knowledge: Community forums are a great place to find solutions and tips that might not be available in official documentation.

- Announcements: Important announcements are often shared in forums, ensuring that active participants are always in the know.

Product Roadmap

ClipCharm's product roadmap is a strategic document that outlines upcoming features, improvements, and long-term goals. Keeping an eye on the roadmap can help you anticipate future updates and plan accordingly.

- *Advantages of Following the Roadmap:*

- Future Planning: Knowing what's coming allows you to plan how to integrate new features into your workflow.

- Feedback Opportunities: Roadmaps often invite user feedback, giving you a chance to influence future developments.

- Transparency: A clear roadmap provides transparency about the direction and priorities of ClipCharm's development.

Beta Programs

Joining ClipCharm's beta programs can give you early access to new features and updates before they are released to the general public. This can be particularly useful for power users who want to stay ahead of the curve.

- *Benefits of Beta Programs:*

  - Early Access: Beta testers get to use new features before anyone else.

  - Feedback Loop: Participating in beta programs allows you to provide feedback that can shape the final release.

  - Experience: Being a beta tester can give you experience with new features that you can share with your team or community.

Third-Party Blogs and Tech News Websites

In addition to official sources, many third-party blogs and technology news websites cover ClipCharm updates and news. Following reputable tech blogs and websites can provide additional perspectives and insights.

- *Why Follow Third-Party Sources?*

  - Independent Reviews: Third-party sources often provide independent reviews and analyses that can offer a different perspective.

  - Comparisons: These sources might compare ClipCharm with other tools, helping you understand its relative strengths and weaknesses.

  - Broader Context: Tech news websites place ClipCharm updates in the broader context of industry trends and developments.

Podcasts and YouTube Channels

Many tech enthusiasts and professionals share their insights through podcasts and YouTube channels. Following content creators who focus on productivity tools and software can be an engaging way to stay updated.

- Advantages of Podcasts and YouTube:

- Convenient Consumption: Podcasts can be listened to on the go, making it easy to stay informed even with a busy schedule.

- Visual Learning: YouTube channels often include video tutorials and demonstrations, which can be very helpful for visual learners.

- Community Engagement: These platforms often have active comment sections where viewers can discuss content and share insights.

ClipCharm User Groups and Meetups

Joining ClipCharm user groups and attending meetups can provide direct access to a community of users who share your interest in the tool. These groups often share news and updates as part of their activities.

- Benefits of User Groups and Meetups:

- Networking: Meetups provide an opportunity to network with other ClipCharm users and experts.

- Shared Learning: User groups often organize events, webinars, and discussions that are valuable for continuous learning.

- Local Focus: Some user groups focus on specific regions, offering localized support and information.

Official Documentation and Release Notes

ClipCharm's official documentation and release notes are comprehensive resources for understanding new features and updates. Regularly reviewing these documents can ensure that you are fully aware of all changes and improvements.

- Importance of Official Documentation:

- Detailed Information: Official documentation provides detailed descriptions and instructions for new features.

- Accuracy: Release notes are the most accurate source of information about updates and bug fixes.

- Reference: These documents can be a valuable reference when you need to understand specific aspects of the tool.

Press Releases

ClipCharm's press releases often announce major updates, partnerships, and strategic changes. Subscribing to a news service that includes press releases or checking ClipCharm's press release section on their website can keep you informed about significant developments.

- *Why Follow Press Releases?*

- Major Announcements: Press releases often include major announcements that are not covered in other channels.

- Official Statements: These documents provide official statements and positions from ClipCharm.

- Media Coverage: Press releases often lead to media coverage, providing additional insights and analyses.

7.2.2 Following ClipCharm on Social Media

In the digital age, social media platforms have become essential tools for staying updated on the latest developments, features, and trends related to software and technology. Following ClipCharm on social media is a strategic way to remain informed about updates, get tips and tricks, and engage with a community of users who share your interests. This section will explore the various social media platforms where ClipCharm is active, the type of content you can expect, and how to effectively use these platforms to enhance your ClipCharm experience.

Importance of Social Media for Software Users

Social media serves as a dynamic and interactive channel for software companies to communicate with their users. By following ClipCharm on social media, users can:

- Receive Instant Updates: Social media platforms often serve as the first point of contact for announcing new features, updates, and bug fixes. This ensures that users are always in the loop regarding the latest enhancements and can adapt their workflows accordingly.

- Access Educational Content: Many companies share tutorials, how-to guides, and best practices on their social media pages. This content can help users learn new functionalities and improve their proficiency with the software.

- Engage with the Community: Social media provides a platform for users to connect with other ClipCharm enthusiasts, share experiences, and seek advice. This sense of community can be invaluable for troubleshooting and discovering new ways to use the software.

- Provide Feedback: Users can directly communicate with the ClipCharm team, offering feedback and suggestions for future updates. This interaction can help shape the development of the software to better meet user needs.

Platforms to Follow ClipCharm

ClipCharm maintains an active presence on several social media platforms, each offering unique content and engagement opportunities. Here are the primary platforms you should consider following:

Facebook

- Page and Group: ClipCharm's Facebook page is a hub for announcements, feature highlights, and user stories. The page often shares videos, articles, and tips that can help you get the most out of ClipCharm. Additionally, many users join ClipCharm-related Facebook groups where they can ask questions, share insights, and connect with other users.

- Engagement: Follow the ClipCharm Facebook page and join relevant groups to stay updated and participate in discussions. Engage with posts by liking, commenting, and sharing your experiences.

Twitter

- Official Account: ClipCharm's Twitter account is a great source for real-time updates. Tweets often include news about upcoming features, maintenance schedules, and quick tips. The platform's fast-paced nature makes it ideal for staying current with the latest information.

- Hashtags and Mentions: Use and follow relevant hashtags such as ClipCharm and Microsoft365 to find user-generated content and participate in broader conversations. Mention @ClipCharm in your tweets to directly communicate with the team or share your insights.

LinkedIn

- Company Page: LinkedIn is an excellent platform for more in-depth professional content. Follow ClipCharm's LinkedIn page for detailed articles, case studies, and updates that are geared towards business users and professionals.

- Networking: Connect with ClipCharm experts and other users in your industry. Participate in LinkedIn groups and discussions to expand your professional network and learn from others' experiences.

YouTube

- Official Channel: ClipCharm's YouTube channel is a rich resource for video content, including tutorials, webinars, and feature overviews. Videos are a highly effective way to learn visually and understand complex functionalities.

- Subscription: Subscribe to the ClipCharm YouTube channel and enable notifications to be alerted whenever new videos are uploaded. Engage with the content by liking, commenting, and sharing videos that you find helpful.

Instagram

- Visual Content: ClipCharm's Instagram account offers a more visual approach, showcasing user stories, feature highlights, and behind-the-scenes content. This platform is ideal for users who prefer visual learning and want to see practical examples of ClipCharm in action.

- Engagement: Follow the ClipCharm Instagram account and engage with posts by liking and commenting. Use Instagram Stories and IGTV for quick tips and updates.

Reddit

- Subreddit: The ClipCharm subreddit is a community-driven space where users can post questions, share tips, and discuss various aspects of the software. It's an excellent place for peer-to-peer support and discovering user-generated solutions.

- Participation: Join the subreddit, follow threads that interest you, and contribute by asking questions or providing answers. Upvote helpful posts to support community engagement.

How to Effectively Use Social Media for ClipCharm Updates

To maximize the benefits of following ClipCharm on social media, consider the following tips:

1. Set Notifications: Ensure you have notifications enabled for ClipCharm's social media accounts. This way, you'll receive instant alerts for new posts and updates, keeping you informed without having to constantly check the platforms.

2. Engage Actively: Don't just passively consume content. Engage with posts by liking, commenting, and sharing. This not only helps you retain information better but also supports the community and increases the visibility of useful content.

3. Join Groups and Forums: Participate in relevant groups and forums on Facebook, LinkedIn, and Reddit. These spaces are often where the most valuable user-generated content and discussions take place.

4. Use Hashtags: On platforms like Twitter and Instagram, use and follow relevant hashtags to discover additional content and engage in broader conversations about ClipCharm.

5. Share Your Insights: Contribute your own experiences and tips. By sharing what you've learned, you help build the community and establish yourself as a knowledgeable user.

6. Stay Professional: While social media is informal, maintaining a professional demeanor when interacting with the ClipCharm community reflects well on you and encourages productive conversations.

Benefits of Following ClipCharm on Social Media

By actively following and engaging with ClipCharm on social media, you can enjoy several benefits:

- Timely Updates: Be the first to know about new features, updates, and maintenance schedules, allowing you to plan and adapt accordingly.

- Learning Opportunities: Access a wealth of educational content, from quick tips to in-depth tutorials, helping you improve your skills and use ClipCharm more effectively.

- Community Support: Gain insights from a community of users who may have encountered and solved the same challenges you face. This peer support can be invaluable for troubleshooting and discovering new functionalities.

- Direct Communication: Engage directly with the ClipCharm team, providing feedback, asking questions, and suggesting improvements. This direct line of communication can influence the development of features that better meet user needs.

- Enhanced Collaboration: Connect with other ClipCharm users, share best practices, and collaborate on projects, enhancing your overall productivity and efficiency.

Conclusion

Following ClipCharm on social media is a strategic and effective way to stay informed, learn new skills, and connect with a community of users. By leveraging the diverse content and engagement opportunities across platforms like Facebook, Twitter, LinkedIn, YouTube, Instagram, and Reddit, you can enhance your ClipCharm experience and ensure you are always up-to-date with the latest developments. Active participation and engagement not only benefit you but also contribute to a vibrant and supportive ClipCharm community.

Appendix

A.1 Glossary of Terms

In this section, we provide definitions and explanations for various terms and concepts related to ClipCharm and Microsoft 365. This glossary aims to enhance your understanding and facilitate your use of the software effectively.

Access Control

Access control refers to the process of granting or restricting specific users' ability to view or manipulate data and functionalities within ClipCharm or Microsoft 365. This is crucial for maintaining data security and ensuring that only authorized personnel can perform certain actions.

Automation

Automation in ClipCharm involves setting up rules or workflows that automatically perform tasks based on predefined triggers. This can include generating clips, organizing content, or integrating with other Microsoft 365 applications to streamline processes and increase efficiency.

Clip

A clip is a basic unit of content within ClipCharm. It can consist of text, images, videos, or other media that can be created, edited, and organized within the software. Clips can be used for various purposes such as tutorials, presentations, or documentation.

Clip Library

The clip library is a repository within ClipCharm where all created clips are stored. Users can organize their clips in the library by categorizing, tagging, and using folders to maintain a well-structured collection of content.

Collaboration

Collaboration in ClipCharm refers to the ability of multiple users to work together on creating, editing, and managing clips. This feature is essential for team projects, allowing for shared access and real-time updates to clips.

Dashboard

The dashboard is the main interface of ClipCharm where users can access their clips, projects, and tools. It provides an overview of recent activities, quick access to important functions, and a centralized hub for managing all ClipCharm-related tasks.

Integration

Integration involves connecting ClipCharm with other Microsoft 365 tools like Word, Excel, Teams, and SharePoint. This enables users to seamlessly incorporate clips into their documents, spreadsheets, and collaborative spaces, enhancing overall productivity.

Metadata

Metadata is the data that describes and provides information about other data. In ClipCharm, metadata includes details such as the clip's title, tags, creation date, author, and other attributes that help in organizing and searching for clips.

Microsoft 365

Microsoft 365 is a suite of productivity applications that includes Word, Excel, PowerPoint, Outlook, Teams, and other tools designed to enhance collaboration and efficiency in a professional setting. ClipCharm integrates with Microsoft 365 to leverage these tools for creating and managing clips.

Project

A project in ClipCharm is a collection of related clips and other media that are grouped together for a specific purpose. Projects help users organize their work, making it easier to manage and track progress on complex tasks.

Tagging

Tagging involves assigning descriptive keywords to clips within ClipCharm. Tags help in categorizing and searching for clips, making it easier to locate specific content quickly.

Template

A template in ClipCharm is a pre-designed layout or structure that users can apply to new clips to ensure consistency and save time. Templates can include predefined text, images, formatting, and other elements that streamline the clip creation process.

User Interface (UI)

The user interface (UI) of ClipCharm refers to the visual elements and layout through which users interact with the software. A well-designed UI is intuitive, making it easy for users to navigate and utilize ClipCharm's features effectively.

Workflow

A workflow in ClipCharm is a sequence of tasks or actions that are automated to achieve a specific outcome. Workflows can be customized to perform repetitive tasks, ensuring consistency and efficiency in clip management.

Collaboration Tools

Collaboration tools in Microsoft 365 include applications like Teams and SharePoint that facilitate communication and teamwork. ClipCharm integrates with these tools to enable users to share and collaborate on clips within their teams.

Version Control

Version control in ClipCharm involves tracking and managing changes to clips over time. This ensures that users can access previous versions of a clip, monitor edits, and revert to earlier versions if necessary.

Cloud Storage

Cloud storage refers to the practice of storing data on remote servers accessed via the internet. ClipCharm utilizes cloud storage to ensure that clips are securely stored, easily accessible, and can be shared with others without the limitations of local storage.

Permissions

Permissions in ClipCharm determine what actions a user can perform on a clip or within a project. This includes viewing, editing, deleting, or sharing clips, ensuring that access is controlled and secure.

Multi-User Access

Multi-user access allows multiple individuals to access and work on the same clip or project simultaneously. This feature is essential for collaborative environments where teamwork and real-time updates are crucial.

Customization

Customization in ClipCharm involves tailoring the software settings, templates, and workflows to meet specific user needs. This ensures that ClipCharm aligns with individual or organizational preferences and enhances usability.

Search Functionality

Search functionality in ClipCharm enables users to quickly locate clips using keywords, tags, metadata, and other criteria. An efficient search function is vital for managing large clip libraries and retrieving information promptly.

Export Options

Export options in ClipCharm allow users to save clips in various formats for use outside the software. This can include exporting to PDF, Word, or directly integrating clips into other Microsoft 365 applications.

Import Options

Import options in ClipCharm enable users to bring external content into the software. This can include importing media files, documents, or data from other applications to create comprehensive and integrated clips.

Security Features

Security features in ClipCharm ensure that clips and data are protected from unauthorized access and breaches. This includes encryption, secure access controls, and compliance with data protection regulations.

Real-Time Collaboration

Real-time collaboration refers to the ability of multiple users to work on a clip simultaneously, with updates being reflected instantaneously. This feature enhances teamwork and productivity in collaborative projects.

User Roles

User roles in ClipCharm define the level of access and permissions assigned to different users. Roles can include administrators, editors, and viewers, each with specific capabilities within the software.

Activity Log

The activity log in ClipCharm records all actions performed within the software, providing a detailed history of changes, edits, and user interactions. This log is crucial for tracking progress and maintaining accountability.

Productivity Tools

Productivity tools in Microsoft 365, such as Word, Excel, and PowerPoint, are integrated with ClipCharm to enhance the clip creation and management process. These tools provide additional functionalities that complement ClipCharm's features.

Compliance

Compliance in ClipCharm involves adhering to legal and regulatory standards for data management and security. This includes ensuring that clips and user data are handled in accordance with applicable laws and industry guidelines.

File Management

File management in ClipCharm involves organizing, storing, and maintaining clips and associated media. Effective file management ensures that content is easily accessible and well-organized.

Scalability

Scalability refers to ClipCharm's ability to handle increasing amounts of data and users as an organization grows. A scalable system ensures that ClipCharm remains efficient and effective even as demands increase.

User Support

User support in ClipCharm includes resources and assistance provided to users to help them navigate and utilize the software. This can include tutorials, help guides, and customer support services.

Onboarding

Onboarding in ClipCharm involves the process of introducing and training new users on how to use the software. Effective onboarding ensures that users are quickly up to speed and able to leverage ClipCharm's features.

Reporting

Reporting in ClipCharm involves generating summaries and insights based on clip usage and activity. This helps users track performance, identify trends, and make informed decisions.

Updates

Updates in ClipCharm refer to software improvements and new feature releases that enhance functionality and address issues. Staying updated ensures that users benefit from the latest advancements and improvements.

User Experience (UX)

User experience (UX) in ClipCharm refers to the overall experience of users when interacting with the software. A positive UX is achieved through intuitive design, responsive performance, and user-friendly features.

Templates Library

The templates library in ClipCharm is a collection of pre-designed templates that users can utilize to create consistent and professional clips. Access to a variety of templates helps streamline the creation process.

Analytics

Analytics in ClipCharm involve tracking and analyzing data related to clip usage, user interaction, and performance. Analytics provide valuable insights that can guide improvements and optimize workflows.

Backup and Recovery

Backup and recovery in ClipCharm involve protecting clip data by creating copies that can be restored in case of data loss. This ensures that important content is not permanently lost due to technical issues or errors.

Bookmark

A bookmark in ClipCharm allows users to mark a specific location within a clip for easy access later. This is useful for quickly navigating to important sections of content.

Cloud Sync

Cloud sync refers to the process of automatically updating and synchronizing clips and data between ClipCharm and cloud storage services. This ensures that users always have access to the most current version of their clips from any device.

Cross-Platform Compatibility

Cross-platform compatibility means that ClipCharm can be used on different operating systems and devices, such as Windows, macOS, iOS, and Android. This flexibility allows users to work on their clips from various devices seamlessly.

Data Encryption

Data encryption in ClipCharm ensures that information is converted into a secure format that can only be accessed by authorized users. This is crucial for protecting sensitive data and maintaining privacy.

Drag-and-Drop

The drag-and-drop feature in ClipCharm allows users to easily move or organize clips and other elements by clicking and dragging them to the desired location. This intuitive functionality enhances ease of use.

Embedded Content

Embedded content refers to media or other elements that are integrated into a clip within ClipCharm. This can include videos, audio files, links, and documents that enrich the content.

Export Formats

Export formats in ClipCharm refer to the various file types in which clips can be saved and exported, such as PDF, DOCX, PPTX, and more. This flexibility ensures that clips can be used in different applications and contexts.

Feedback Loop

A feedback loop in ClipCharm involves collecting and incorporating user feedback to improve clips and workflows. This iterative process helps refine content and enhance user satisfaction.

File Sharing

File sharing in ClipCharm enables users to share clips and associated files with others via links, email, or cloud services. This feature supports collaboration and content dissemination.

Hyperlink

A hyperlink in ClipCharm is a clickable link that directs users to external websites, documents, or other clips. Hyperlinks enhance navigation and provide quick access to related information.

Layout

The layout in ClipCharm refers to the arrangement of elements within a clip, such as text, images, and media. Effective layout design improves readability and visual appeal.

Multi-Device Access

Multi-device access allows users to work on ClipCharm clips from multiple devices, such as desktops, laptops, tablets, and smartphones. This ensures flexibility and convenience in managing clips.

Notification

Notifications in ClipCharm alert users to important updates, changes, or actions required within the software. These can include reminders, task updates, and collaboration invitations.

Offline Access

Offline access in ClipCharm enables users to work on clips without an internet connection. Changes made offline are synchronized with the cloud once connectivity is restored.

Permissions Management

Permissions management in ClipCharm involves configuring and controlling the access rights of different users to clips and projects. This ensures that only authorized individuals can view or edit content.

Preview Mode

Preview mode in ClipCharm allows users to see how a clip will appear to others before finalizing and sharing it. This helps ensure that content is polished and free of errors.

Quick Access Toolbar

The quick access toolbar in ClipCharm provides users with shortcuts to frequently used tools and functions. Customizing this toolbar can streamline workflow and improve efficiency.

Revision History

Revision history in ClipCharm tracks all changes made to a clip over time. Users can view previous versions, compare changes, and restore earlier versions if needed.

Sharing Settings

Sharing settings in ClipCharm allow users to control how and with whom clips are shared. This includes setting permissions, expiry dates for links, and restricting access.

Snippet

A snippet in ClipCharm is a small, reusable piece of content that can be quickly inserted into clips. Snippets save time by allowing users to reuse standard text or media elements.

Task Management

Task management in ClipCharm involves assigning, tracking, and managing tasks related to clip creation and editing. This ensures that projects are completed efficiently and on schedule.

Text Formatting

Text formatting in ClipCharm includes options for customizing the appearance of text, such as font size, color, style, and alignment. Proper formatting enhances readability and presentation.

Thumbnail

A thumbnail in ClipCharm is a small preview image that represents a clip. Thumbnails help users quickly identify and navigate to specific clips within their library.

Time Stamps

Time stamps in ClipCharm indicate the date and time when a clip was created or modified. This information is useful for tracking changes and managing content timelines.

Two-Factor Authentication (2FA)

Two-factor authentication (2FA) adds an extra layer of security to ClipCharm accounts by requiring users to verify their identity through a second method, such as a code sent to their phone.

User Manual

The user manual in ClipCharm provides comprehensive instructions and guidelines on how to use the software. This resource is essential for new users to get acquainted with ClipCharm's features.

Video Clips

Video clips in ClipCharm are segments of video content that can be created, edited, and managed within the software. These clips can be used for tutorials, presentations, and other multimedia purposes.

Virtual Workspace

A virtual workspace in ClipCharm is an online environment where users can create, edit, and collaborate on clips. This space is accessible from anywhere with an internet connection, facilitating remote work.

Web Integration

Web integration in ClipCharm refers to the ability to embed web content and interact with web services directly within the software. This enhances functionality and connectivity.

Widget

A widget in ClipCharm is a small application or tool that provides specific functionality, such as a calendar, to-do list, or media player. Widgets enhance the user experience by adding useful features.

Workflow Optimization

Workflow optimization in ClipCharm involves refining and streamlining processes to improve efficiency and productivity. This includes automating repetitive tasks and eliminating bottlenecks.

XML

XML (eXtensible Markup Language) in ClipCharm is a format used for encoding documents and data. XML files can be used to import and export structured information within the software.

Zoom Function

The zoom function in ClipCharm allows users to magnify or reduce the view of their clips. This is useful for detailed editing and ensuring that content is clear and legible.

By understanding these terms, you can better navigate and utilize ClipCharm within Microsoft 365, making the most of its features and capabilities. This glossary serves as a valuable reference for both new and experienced users, helping to demystify the terminology and enhance your overall experience with the software.

A.2 Frequently Asked Questions

Q1: What is ClipCharm?

A1: ClipCharm is a powerful tool integrated into Microsoft 365 that allows users to create, manage, and share multimedia clips and content efficiently. It is designed to enhance productivity and streamline workflows by providing easy-to-use features for content creation and collaboration.

Q2: How do I access ClipCharm in Microsoft 365?

A2: To access ClipCharm, you need to have a Microsoft 365 subscription. Once you have a subscription, you can find ClipCharm in the app launcher (also known as the "waffle" icon) within the Microsoft 365 dashboard. From there, you can launch ClipCharm and start using its features.

Installation and Setup

Q3: How do I install ClipCharm?

A3: ClipCharm is usually pre-installed with your Microsoft 365 subscription. If it is not visible in your app launcher, you may need to contact your IT administrator to enable it for your account. If you are an administrator, you can enable ClipCharm via the Microsoft 365 admin center by assigning it to the appropriate user accounts.

Q4: What are the system requirements for using ClipCharm?

A4: ClipCharm is a web-based application and requires an internet connection to function. It is compatible with most modern web browsers, including Chrome, Firefox, Edge, and Safari. Ensure that your browser is up-to-date to avoid compatibility issues. Additionally, ClipCharm performs best with a stable and high-speed internet connection.

Q5: Can I use ClipCharm on mobile devices?

A5: Yes, ClipCharm is accessible on mobile devices through the Microsoft 365 mobile app. The mobile version provides a user-friendly interface optimized for touchscreens, allowing you to create, edit, and manage clips on the go. Ensure you have the latest version of the Microsoft 365 app installed on your device.

Basic Features and Usage

Q6: How do I create a new clip in ClipCharm?

A6: To create a new clip in ClipCharm, follow these steps:

1. Open ClipCharm from the Microsoft 365 app launcher.

2. Click on the "Create New Clip" button.

3. Use the provided tools to add multimedia elements such as text, images, audio, and video.

4. Customize your clip using the editing options available.

5. Save your clip by clicking the "Save" button.

Q7: How do I organize my clips?

A7: You can organize your clips in ClipCharm by creating folders and subfolders. To create a folder, click on the "New Folder" button, name your folder, and drag your clips into it. Use descriptive names and categorize your clips based on projects, topics, or dates to keep your library organized.

Q8: Can I share my clips with others?

A8: Yes, ClipCharm allows you to share your clips with others. You can share clips directly with colleagues via email or by generating a shareable link. Additionally, you can set permissions to control whether recipients can view, comment, or edit your clips. Use the sharing options to collaborate effectively with your team.

Advanced Features

Q9: What automation features are available in ClipCharm?

A9: ClipCharm offers several automation features to streamline your workflow. These include:

- Automation Rules: Set up rules to automate repetitive tasks, such as organizing clips or sending notifications.

- Workflow Integration: Integrate ClipCharm with other Microsoft 365 tools like Teams and SharePoint to automate content sharing and collaboration.

- Templates: Use pre-designed templates to quickly create consistent and professional clips.

Q10: How do I integrate ClipCharm with other Microsoft 365 tools?

A10: ClipCharm integrates seamlessly with other Microsoft 365 tools. To integrate with tools like Word, Excel, Teams, and SharePoint:

1. Open ClipCharm and select the clip you want to integrate.

2. Click on the "Share" button and choose the tool you want to integrate with.

3. Follow the prompts to complete the integration process.

This allows you to embed clips in documents, share them in team channels, and collaborate across different platforms.

Troubleshooting

Q11: What should I do if ClipCharm is not loading?

A11: If ClipCharm is not loading, try the following troubleshooting steps:

1. Ensure your internet connection is stable.

2. Clear your browser cache and cookies.

3. Check if your browser is up-to-date.

4. Disable any browser extensions that might be interfering.

5. Restart your browser or try accessing ClipCharm from a different browser.

If the issue persists, contact your IT support or Microsoft 365 support for further assistance.

Q12: How do I recover a deleted clip?

A12: To recover a deleted clip in ClipCharm:

1. Go to the "Deleted Items" folder in ClipCharm.

2. Locate the clip you want to recover.

3. Select the clip and click on the "Restore" button.

If the clip is not in the "Deleted Items" folder, it might have been permanently deleted, and recovery options will depend on your organization's data retention policies.

Q13: Why am I unable to share a clip with external users?

A13: Sharing clips with external users may be restricted by your organization's settings. Check with your IT administrator to ensure external sharing is enabled. Additionally, ensure that the external user's email address is correct and that you have set the appropriate sharing permissions.

Customization and Personalization

Q14: Can I customize the ClipCharm interface?

A14: Yes, ClipCharm allows for some level of customization. You can personalize your workspace by adjusting the layout, color scheme, and display settings. Access the customization options in the settings menu to make changes that suit your preferences.

Q15: How do I set up notification preferences in ClipCharm?

A15: To set up notification preferences in ClipCharm:

1. Go to the settings menu.

2. Navigate to the "Notifications" section.

3. Choose the types of notifications you want to receive (e.g., email alerts, in-app notifications).

4. Customize the frequency and channels for notifications.

This helps you stay informed about updates, collaboration activities, and other important events.

Best Practices

Q16: What are some best practices for using ClipCharm effectively?

A16: To use ClipCharm effectively, consider the following best practices:

- Organize Clips: Use folders and tags to keep your clips organized.

- Collaborate: Share clips with team members and use collaboration features to enhance productivity.

- Automate: Take advantage of automation rules to streamline repetitive tasks.

- Update Regularly: Keep your clips up-to-date to ensure relevance and accuracy.

- Backup: Regularly backup your clips to avoid data loss.

Q17: How can I improve my clip creation process?

A17: To improve your clip creation process:

1. Plan Ahead: Outline the content and structure of your clip before you start creating.

2. Use Templates: Utilize templates to maintain consistency and save time.

3. Incorporate Multimedia: Add images, videos, and audio to make your clips more engaging.

4. Edit Thoroughly: Review and edit your clips to ensure clarity and quality.

5. Seek Feedback: Share drafts with colleagues for feedback and improvements.

Security and Privacy

Q18: How secure is my data in ClipCharm?

A18: ClipCharm adheres to Microsoft 365's robust security and privacy standards. Your data is encrypted both in transit and at rest, ensuring it is protected against unauthorized access. Additionally, Microsoft 365 offers advanced security features such as multi-factor authentication, data loss prevention, and compliance certifications to safeguard your information.

Q19: How can I control access to my clips?

A19: You can control access to your clips by setting permissions for each clip or folder. In the sharing settings, specify whether users can view, comment, or edit your clips. You can also restrict access to specific individuals or groups, ensuring that only authorized users can access your content.

Q20: What should I do if I suspect a security breach in ClipCharm?

A20: If you suspect a security breach in ClipCharm:

1. Change Passwords: Immediately change your Microsoft 365 account password.

2. Review Activity: Check recent activity in ClipCharm for any suspicious actions.

3. Contact IT Support: Report the suspected breach to your IT support team.

4. Follow Security Protocols: Follow your organization's security protocols to mitigate any potential damage.

Learning and Support

Q21: Where can I find tutorials and training for ClipCharm?

A21: Tutorials and training for ClipCharm can be found on the Microsoft 365 support website, which offers a variety of resources, including video tutorials, user guides, and webinars. Additionally, you can join the ClipCharm user community for peer-to-peer learning and support.

Q22: How can I provide feedback or suggestions for ClipCharm?

A22: You can provide feedback or suggestions for ClipCharm through the Microsoft 365 feedback portal. In ClipCharm, navigate to the "Help" or "Feedback" section, where you can submit your comments. Your feedback helps improve the tool and address any user concerns.

Updates and Future Developments

Q23: How do I stay informed about updates to ClipCharm?

A23: Stay informed about updates to ClipCharm by:

- Subscribing to Newsletters: Sign up for Microsoft 365 newsletters and update notifications.

- Following Official Channels: Follow Microsoft 365 and ClipCharm on social media platforms.

- Checking Release Notes: Regularly check the release notes in ClipCharm for information about new features and updates.

Q24: What are some upcoming features in ClipCharm?

A24: Microsoft continuously works on enhancing ClipCharm with new features and improvements. Upcoming features may include advanced editing tools, improved integration with other Microsoft 365 apps, enhanced collaboration capabilities, and more automation options. Keep an eye on official announcements for the latest updates.

A.3 Conclusion

As we reach the end of "ClipCharm for Beginners: A Step-by-Step Guide in Microsoft 365," it's important to reflect on the journey we've taken together. This book was designed to be a comprehensive introduction to ClipCharm, aiming to transform you from a novice into a confident user of this powerful tool within the Microsoft 365 ecosystem. Let's take a moment to summarize the key points we've covered and consider the impact ClipCharm can have on your productivity and collaboration efforts.

Recap of Key Concepts

Throughout this guide, we've explored the various facets of ClipCharm, starting with the basics and progressively delving into more advanced features. Here's a brief recap of what we've covered:

- Introduction to ClipCharm and Microsoft 365: We began by defining ClipCharm and highlighting its role within Microsoft 365. Understanding its key features and benefits laid the foundation for appreciating how ClipCharm can enhance your workflow.

- Getting Started: Setting up ClipCharm, navigating its interface, and grasping the basic functions are crucial first steps. We provided a detailed guide on installation, initial configuration, and creating your first clips.

- Content Creation: Creating and managing clips effectively is the heart of ClipCharm usage. We walked you through the steps of clip creation, customization, and organization, ensuring you can maintain a streamlined clip library.

- Advanced Features: Integration with other Microsoft 365 tools, automation of tasks, and customization of settings allow for a more sophisticated use of ClipCharm. We explored these features to help you maximize ClipCharm's potential.

- Best Practices: We shared strategies for organizing clips, enhancing collaboration, and maintaining your clip library. These best practices are designed to help you use ClipCharm efficiently and effectively.

- Troubleshooting and Support: No tool is without its challenges. We provided solutions to common issues and highlighted the available support resources to ensure you can overcome any obstacles you encounter.

The Impact of ClipCharm on Productivity

ClipCharm is more than just a tool; it's a catalyst for productivity and collaboration. By integrating ClipCharm into your daily workflow, you can streamline content creation, enhance team collaboration, and maintain an organized repository of resources. Here are some specific ways ClipCharm can impact your work:

- Efficiency: ClipCharm simplifies the process of creating and managing clips, saving you time and effort. By organizing clips efficiently and using automation features, you can focus on more critical tasks.

- Collaboration: Sharing clips with team members and collaborating on projects in real-time fosters a more cohesive working environment. ClipCharm's integration with Microsoft 365 tools like Teams and SharePoint enhances this collaborative potential.

- Consistency: By using templates and standardized clips, you can ensure consistency across your documents and presentations. This is particularly beneficial for maintaining brand integrity and professional standards.

- Organization: A well-organized clip library makes it easy to find and reuse content, reducing redundancy and improving overall productivity. ClipCharm's search and filtering features are invaluable in this regard.

Future Prospects

The future of ClipCharm within the Microsoft 365 ecosystem looks promising. With regular updates and new features, ClipCharm continues to evolve, offering even more ways to enhance productivity and collaboration. Staying informed about these developments will ensure you can take full advantage of the latest enhancements.

- Upcoming Features: Keep an eye out for new features and updates from the ClipCharm team. These may include improved integration with other tools, enhanced automation capabilities, and additional customization options.

- Industry Trends: As digital collaboration and remote work continue to grow, tools like ClipCharm will become increasingly important. Understanding industry trends can help you anticipate changes and adapt your workflow accordingly.

- Continued Learning: Engage with the ClipCharm user community and explore additional resources to continue learning and improving your ClipCharm skills. Online courses, tutorials, and forums are excellent ways to stay up-to-date and connected.

Final Thoughts

Dear Reader,

Thank you for choosing "ClipCharm for Beginners: A Step-by-Step Guide in Microsoft 365." Your decision to delve into the world of ClipCharm and Microsoft 365 is greatly appreciated, and I am truly honored to be part of your journey toward mastering these powerful tools.

Writing this book has been a rewarding experience, and I am thrilled to share the insights, tips, and techniques that will help you make the most of ClipCharm. Your support is invaluable, and it motivates me to continue providing useful and engaging content.

I hope this guide proves to be a valuable resource as you explore and utilize ClipCharm to enhance your productivity and efficiency. Should you have any feedback or suggestions, please feel free to reach out. Your input helps me improve and ensures that future editions of this book will meet your needs even better.

Thank you once again for your trust and support. Wishing you success and satisfaction in your ClipCharm journey!

Warm regards,

www.ingramcontent.com/pod-product-compliance
Lightning Source LLC
LaVergne TN
LVHW081340050326
832903LV00024B/1240